MW01166305

Cruising at 30,000 Feet

BONNIE LISS

A Young Widow's Personal Account of a

MACMILLAN   PUBLISHING

CRUISING AT 30,000 FEET

Year of Readjustment, Recovery, and Renewal

CO ., INC.   *New York*

Macmillan Publishing Co., Inc.
866 Third Avenue, New York, N.Y. 10022
Collier Macmillan Canada, Inc.

Library of Congress Cataloging in Publication Data

Liss, Bonnie.
    Cruising at 30,000 feet.

    1. Widows—United States—Biography.   2. Women
architects—United States—Biography.   I. Title.
II. Title: Cruising at thirty thousand feet.
HQ1058.5.U5L55   1983   306.8'8 [B]   82-21704
ISBN 0-02-572980-2

10 9 8 7 6 5 4 3 2 1

Printed in the United States of America

For Miles, Seth, and Asher

I want to thank my friends Leon and Stephanie Rosenblatt for their support, literary criticism, and Caesar salads.

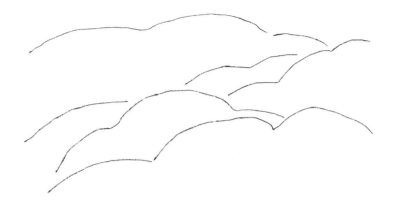

PART ONE

1

The sun was rising over the south Florida Atlantic, cutting through a curtain of clouds with the vengeance it always has on August mornings. I was rising faster in a Boeing 727 on my way to Atlanta.

"We would like to welcome you to today's flight number 710, nonstop service to Atlanta, with continuing service to Charlotte."

The senior flight attendant read into the mike, while another performed the takeoff mime, demonstrating all of the emergency escape measures. She was totally animated and cheerful and fully made-up. It was 6:20 A.M., and nobody was watching. The entire first-class cabin was in a predawn daze except for me. I watched her with the absolute interest of someone very much in need of an emergency escape measure.

"This morning's flight will take an hour and forty-seven minutes. As soon as we reach our cruising altitude of thirty thousand feet, the captain will turn off the seat-belt signs and you will be free to move about the cabin. On behalf of

3

the entire crew, I would like to thank you for choosing to fly with us this morning."

The plane was full of company employees. Flight #710 is known as the pass-rider's special. It leaves Miami early in the morning, and most paying passengers are tourists who don't want to leave before the checkout time in their hotels. They have paid to stay until noon and, Goddamn it, they are going to stay until noon and get that last blast of sun on their bodies. So, day after day the afternoon flight out of Miami is full of tourists, and flight #710 is full of company employees traveling on business or for pleasure.

That day I was an employee traveling on business. My business was housing all the facilities that make it possible for a person to get into a hunk of metal at point A, go up in the air, and come down at point B.

"You're an architect for an airline?" I'm often asked. "What do they need architects for? What do you design?"

It has never been a town house. On that day it was a ticket office in a suburban Atlanta Hilton Hotel—my first actual project in my first actual job.

"No big deal, Bonnie—a piece of cake," the senior project architect said as he handed me the construction file. "Just check the plans with the space, make sure it'll work. But it will work, because I designed it myself. If anything goes wrong, I'll blame you, so don't screw it up, Bonnie, and don't take any crap from the manager at the Hilton. Any questions?"

"No . . . uh, yes. How do I get there?"

"Take a plane," he laughed.

Strapped into my seat, I looked down through the mountains of clouds that were touched pink by the morning light, where Miami stretches out between the swamp and the sea. And then in a few minutes I was above the buildings and above the morning and above, finally above, the confusion of my life, cruising at 30,000 feet.

I had an hour and forty-seven minutes to continue being Bonnie Liss, homemaker, mother, and backseat driver. When the plane landed in Atlanta, I could not be the same person. I would have to be an architect in control.

Flight #710 was my leap of faith. I had never been in a position of authority before. For thirty-five years I had been somebody's little girl. My father had bossed me around, my husband had taken care of things, my kids never took me seriously, and even my dog still peed on the rug. How would I get people to listen to me? What would keep them from laughing or saying "fuck off, Toots"? What if I checked the design plans against the actual space and nothing was right? What if I couldn't tell if it was right or wrong? What if I ran out of the Hilton screaming?

I had been put in touch with the sales manager in Atlanta, who called to let me know that he would meet me Thursday morning outside the terminal to take me to the site. He would be driving a green Datsun.

"What will you be wearing, so I don't pass you by?" he asked.

I thought about stopping him, and said, "a red dress"; after he hung up I realized that my only red dress was a winter dress and this was August. I wore it anyway because I didn't want to confuse him and because I knew that I would be so anxious about the whole thing that wearing a winter dress wouldn't make much difference.

But what if he just forgot to pick me up, or what if he didn't drive up in his green Datsun, or what if he just drove by the lady sweating like a pig in her red dress? What would I do? How long was I supposed to stand on the curb in the hot Georgia sun, waiting for a man I didn't know to take me to a job I wasn't familiar with, where I would have to tell men I didn't know what was necessary to make it work, when at that point I was absolutely positive that it wouldn't work.

As we got closer to Atlanta, I was also absolutely positive that nobody would be there to pick me up. What would be the professional thing to do? Could I leave after I waited an hour? After half an hour? How about five minutes? Should I fly back to Miami? Or just rewrite my ticket and go on to St. Louis and live with my parents, wire for the kids, and mail back my employee badge?

"We are now flying over Lake Okeechobee," the captain announced. "Our route today will be taking us over the Orlando area and then up to Georgia and into Atlanta."

I looked down at the flat Florida landscape and Lake Okeechobee, reminded of what had brought me to where I was. The lake just below looked like a giant and dangerous cell, sprawled flat on a slide under a microscope, waiting to be identified. A cell that they said identified hairy-cell leukemia. A silly name. You could almost visualize the cell as a cartoon character—Hemo the Magnificent, Harry the Cell. It had killed my husband, Bob, six weeks before.

The son of a bitch, I thought, the nerve of him to die and leave me alone.

Then I felt rotten for thinking that, because, of course, he had no choice about dying so young. But that single fact had pushed me into actions I had never intended taking. I was the nonswimmer going off the high dive, and I didn't know if I would splash or splat or ever make it back to the locker room.

"Will you be having breakfast with us?" the stewardess asked.

When I said yes she pulled down the tray, laid the linen, and served me breakfast. I ate everything. I even ate the parsley and the lettuce that was placed under the orange and pineapple slices. I ate too fast, a habit of most mothers who must wolf down their meals before someone needs more milk or another cookie or starts to cry or misbehaves or wants your food.

I should write a diet book, I thought. "Eat anything you want and lose weight—*The Three-Kids-at-the-Table Diet.* Then I wondered if the kids were up and if Violet, the house-keeper, was giving them breakfast or if they were scrambling for themselves while she watched television. Were they all right? Had I left enough emergency numbers? Was I missed?

My kids were big enough to wake up without me. Miles was eleven, Seth was nine, and Asher eight. But when I thought of them from an altitude of 30,000 feet, they seemed fragile and small. Miles had grown sullen since Bob died. Seth was never home, and Asher seemed to be slowly losing ground. He had been totally nonverbal and was diagnosed as autistic when he was four. But his development had been steady and encouraging until Bob's death.

Did I have to work? Was this really in our best interest? I wondered if I could survive on Social Security. My father would help me out. I really didn't have to work. Just because I had a degree in architecture didn't mean I had to use it or was meant to use it. I could just play the helpless widow and live out my life at somebody else's expense.

But the decision had already been made and I knew that I had opened a door that had closed forever behind me. I had gone into another room—my own room. And if it was all a mistake, and Bob hadn't died, and he came back like Odysseus returning from some awesome journey, I knew that we would have to meet in the hall and find a fresh new room to go into together.

The landscape below had changed from Florida flat to a terrain of pretty green hills with rooftops tucked in under thick trees and ponds gleaming like beacons in the morning sun. The stewardess snatched my tray, and the captain announced that our approach had been cleared into the Atlanta airport.

Charged up with a first-class breakfast and three cups of coffee, I gathered together my carryons, checked my makeup and my seat belt, and was ready for the descent back to earth. This was the beginning of what had really begun six weeks before when a thirty-five-year-old woman, who never worked a day in her life, "awoke one morning from a troubled dream and found [herself] changed in her bed to some monstrous kind of vermin"—a responsible adult.

2

The phone was ringing. The digital numbers on the clock glowed 4:21 A.M., when I lifted the receiver.

"Bonnie, it's Dr. Levin." His familiar voice broke the grip of sleep that was clinging protectively to me.

"Oh, hi, Doctor. What's up?"

I had left my husband in his hospital room a few hours earlier in the last stages of leukemia, and I was actually wondering why his doctor was calling me at four in the morning. Was he calling to cancel an appointment? Had I forgotten to make a payment on my bill? Bob's lingering illness had numbed me. My sensitivities were a flat wave and without legal contest I could have been pronounced emotionally dead.

"Well, I'm sorry to have to tell you this, but Bob's heart stopped."

"Stopped? You mean completely?"

"He died, Bonnie. The resident tried to revive him, but he was gone."

"Gone?"

"Why don't you come in and see me in a few weeks when

everything has settled down. I'm sure you'll have some questions and we'll be able to talk then."

4:21 . . . click, 4:22.

"Wait a minute, wait a minute."

"Yes?"

"Where is he now?"

"He's still in the room at the hospital."

"What do I do now? What do I do?"

"You bury him."

The digital numbers blinked methodically without the courtesy of letting a second slip. I waited until five to wake up my mother, who had come to stay with me five days earlier. She had come to visit Bob and to help me out—to clean the house, to get things in order—and to buy a plot.

"If you don't need it you can sell it back or keep it as an investment," she apologized, thinking she was offending me or bringing bad luck. I tried to read the newspaper while she made the arrangements.

She poked her head into the dining room. "Bonnie, do you want a double plot?"

"Shit, no. One's enough."

"I wouldn't recommend it either. You know, grandpa bought a double plot in Collinsville when his first wife died, and now his second wife is jealous and wants him to buy a double plot for them in St. Louis."

"God, what a decision. Who did he choose?"

"Well, he's such a character. I think he arranged to be buried in Israel, alone."

She went back to close the deal. I went back to my horoscope. "Lie low," it warned.

"They have a few you can look at," she interrupted again. "Do you want to go out there this afternoon and pick one?"

"No. I think I'll lie low today."

"Well, how will they know which one to sell you?"

"Look, Mom, I just want to buy a plot. I don't want to look at it. I'll take the next one in line."

She went back to the phone. "A package deal," I heard her say laughingly from the kitchen, "no, we're not interested in a package deal."

"Mom, Mom," I poked her gently, "Dr. Levin called. Bob died." I wanted to cry but my throat felt frozen, and I could only rasp. "What do I do?" I asked.

"Call his mother."

"I can't. I can't. You do it."

"Okay. Then call the rabbi and the undertaker."

"I can't do that either, Mom. You do it."

"Okay. Why don't you lie down and get some rest."

"I can't."

My mother went downstairs to make the arrangements. I took a hammer and dismantled the hospital bed that waited in the living room for the rare days when Bob had felt well enough to leave the hospital and come home. Then I washed all the floors, got dressed, and sat down to read the manuscript he was working on before he died.

Bob had been a journalist for the *Miami Herald*. When his disease was diagnosed, he had written a series of articles for the *Herald*. On the basis of the articles he got an advance to write a book about dying and about living with that awareness, and he took a leave of absence from the paper to do the book.

I had never read any of the manuscript before. We had an unspoken agreement that I would never read anything he was working on until it was ready to go. He never wanted to feel that a decision he made was a response to my reactions. Once I read something he was working on and started to cry.

"Is it so sad?" he asked in surprise.

"No," I sobbed, "it's so shitty."

He never finished the story. Another time I threatened to divorce him if he didn't change the tone of an article. The only way he could write with me around was by not showing me his pieces until he had reworked and revised without my input. By the time he had a presentation draft, my comments were never very drastic.

So, it wasn't until the morning he died that I picked up the manuscript he had been working on for the month and a half before he went into the hospital, too ill to continue. I couldn't put it down. The story began well and his perceptions were cleverly expressed. It was a strange way to escape the reality of his death—to bury myself in the very story of his dying.

I sat at the dining room table reading as a stream of characters paraded by. They came on like a chorus line, warming up the audience for the finale, building everything up for the funeral, moving me closer and closer to a realization of what had happened.

Rabbi Kramer came on first. He asked me questions about how I wanted the funeral to be handled. I stared at him blankly. I didn't know. I didn't care. A funeral wasn't the kind of social event I had ever spent time thinking about. I had never even been to one. I really just wanted to stay home and read and let them all stick him in the ground if they wanted to, or scatter his ashes at sea, or donate his body to science.

While I sat shuffling through the pages of Bob's book, my mother told him that I wanted the funeral that day and that I wanted a graveside service with the Orthodox traditions observed. I was enjoying the manuscript and found myself laughing with Bob over incidents from our past.

"What about the children?" the rabbi asked.

"Well, Asher's still asleep and Miles and Seth are at

camp. And, I don't know, I don't want to ruin their summer, so why drag them home for a funeral?"

"Okay," said the rabbi, "let me call the camp."

He called. The kids were out on an overnight, and someone went to find them in the woods. Rabbi Kramer drank tea and waited while I continued to read the manuscript. I have always found great solace in reading. I read myself through puberty.

The phone rang and Rabbi Kramer talked to the camp director and came back into the dining room.

"Bonnie," he said, "They found the kids and they're very upset. I think they should come home for the funeral. It will be easier for them if they have that sense of finality. The director is driving them to Atlanta as soon as they change. Can you get them on a plane?"

I had no idea of what he was talking about. A death was a death. How could it be more final? My mother called the airline and explained what had happened. Tickets were expedited and a passenger service representative waited at the airport to get them onto their flight. I kept on reading. My brain was in second gear, my emotions were in park.

Andy Greenberg was on next. He came by from the *Herald* to write the obituary. He asked questions about Bob that I couldn't answer because I couldn't really remember how things were beyond the opaque curtain of his illness. I didn't want the obit to read, "Robert E. Liss, beloved husband and father, who turned gray, got sores on his body, had constant fever and shortness of breath as his blood slowly turned to water, died not so peacefully after a lengthy illness." But those were the only details on my mind. So, I talked about the manuscript and read him a few passages, and when he had enough to construct a story, he made his exit.

Bob's mother, Bernice, entered next. She had gone to the hospital and picked up his personal belongings, which she brought back in one of the hospital's plastic bags. She emptied it out on the dining room table. There were the books he had kept at his bedside table in case he felt strong enough to read. There was the tape recorder he had had to record his thoughts and ideas. The tape was blank—no last message, no philosophizing, no good-bye, no string of curses. There were the cards people had sent him. There were some bottles of aftershave, his slippers and robe, and his wedding ring.

The ring shocked me. Someone had taken it off his finger after he died. I thought he should be buried wearing his ring and his robe and slippers, with his aftershave and tape recorder and books and cards, but I didn't say anything about it. I kept on reading. The pace of the manuscript had slowed to a trickle as he described the hospital procedures. An occasional spurt of satire kept it going.

I could not tear myself away from the book. I could not bring myself to participate in the events at hand. The final act of the play was unfolding on its own, without the leading lady, who did not seem to know her lines and who was indefinitely indisposed. My dining room had become the stage for a play in which I couldn't find my part.

A neighbor came by with a large percolator, a tablecloth, a car, and the ability to organize. She was my mother's understudy. I read the last page of the manuscript. It didn't end; it just piddled out. I searched desperately through his notes for an ending, but there was none. Food trays and flowers began to arrive. The stage was crowded with props and ready for some action.

Asher wandered down all dressed for summer school. I had forgotten that he existed.

"Why didn't you wake me?" he asked. "I'll miss the bus and get in trouble."

His T-shirt was on backward and his socks didn't match. Coaxing my mind into action, I managed to respond.

"You aren't going to school today, Asher."

"Why not?"

"Well, because . . . because your father died." Then I started to cry and so did he.

Judy drove me to the airport to pick up Miles and Seth on our way to the cemetery. Before the kids had gone to camp, I had told them that their father was very sick and that I had no idea how long he would live. But when they got off the plane, I could see that they hadn't understood or believed me. How could they? They lived under a constant media barrage of youthful, healthy, and beautiful images. Sickness was something to cover up, and death was an absolute felony.

"But he had the best doctor," cried Miles, "how could it happen?" He had believed that doctors were holy and was shocked to learn that they really couldn't cure much. Seth looked pale and rumpled. He had thrown up on the plane.

How could I comfort them or handle their grief or answer their questions? I was overcome with stage fright. My inability to act was partly shock and partly grief, but a lot of it was the fact that I hadn't initiated much in the fifteen years of my marriage. Although I had never considered myself dominated, I simply was not the dominant half of the pair. And, suddenly, in this alien situation, I was alone—in charge. Bob was dead, and I was their only adult.

The kids slipped into the back of my neighbor's car and I read her the directions to the cemetery that my mother had neatly written out for us. The directions were simple, but I was overwhelmed with the feeling that I would not, could not, find the place. I, who could find anything, who would wake up suddenly when Bob was driving home late at night after a long trip and say, "Turn here," fall back asleep, and be right about the turn, had lost all confidence in my sense of direction. Even the slightest responsibility was frightening. I was sure that I would not find the way and that we would get lost in the Everglades with two kids bawling in the backseat and a dizzy broad up front who could not decipher her mother's perfect penmanship. We found the cemetery. Everyone was waiting for us. We were the last ones to arrive.

Since it was my first funeral, I wasn't sure about the etiquette. Did I have to shake hands or kiss anybody? Did I have to talk? Would there be a receiving line? Could I scream? The kids were crying next to me. The pine box was suspended over a horrible hole. Was he really in there? I felt totally disoriented—a sleepwalker caught in someone else's nightmare, unable to react or stop it or wake up.

I don't remember too much of the service. It was starkly simple. Rabbi Kramer spoke for a while, and there were some prayers. Half the newsroom of the *Miami Herald* was there. My father and sister Eileen had flown in from St. Louis.

The sky was clear and the heat of the day was breaking. The shadows lengthened as the event drew to a sluggish close. My sister gave a eulogy. She talked about Bob's honesty and curiosity and how they were reflected in the way he lived and died. While she spoke, I thought about how Bob had dragged me into his crazy adventures and wondered what I would do for fun without his curiosity. "He never stopped asking stupid questions" was his requested epitaph.

The cemetery was directly under the landing approach to Miami International Airport, and as the jets came screaming in they interrupted the service and seemed to punctuate the prayers. The piercing sound of an approaching 727 drew me out of my fog, and I looked around at the mourners who were no longer mourning but beginning to shuffle nervously. The rabbi was staring at me, and I realized that he was through.

"What do I do now?" I asked.

"You go home," he said.

"Just like that? I don't have to talk to anybody?"

"No, just go home. I'll come by the house later."

I started to go, but stopped. The coffin was still suspended over the hole and I didn't want to leave until they put it into the ground. I wanted to witness the burial. I needed to hear the thud of earth on the casket so I would be sure it was really all over. And then I realized what Rabbi Kramer had meant by a sense of finality and why it had been important for the kids to be there and why we had all come. It wasn't to "pay our last respects" or to feel shitty. It was to experience the finality of what had happened, to know without a doubt that Bob Liss was no more. He had asked his last question.

I stared at the coffin but didn't have the courage to say anything. Maybe it was supposed to hang there for a while. Maybe it was unorthodox to bury it in public. It wasn't until later, at my grandmother's funeral, that I realized I had been cheated, that the actual burial was a usual part of the process and something I should have demanded. But I was too unsure of myself to request anything. I had to go back a few days later to see if the coffin was still hanging in the air. It wasn't. There was a fresh mound of dirt where the hole had been and a bronze plaque that said Robert E. Liss. But as I stared at the grave I thought, Is he actually in there? I wonder now if I would have had so many awful dreams of Bob alive in the last stages of leukemia if I had actually seen him buried.

"Listen, Rabbi," I appealed, "are you sure it's okay? I mean, I hate to leave him hanging. Are you sure it's all over?"

"Yes, it's over. Go home, Bonnie."

I turned and went to the car. The kids followed me like little ducks.

3

According to Jewish law, the mourner is granted seven days after a death to totally withdraw from daily obligations and to grieve and begin adjusting to life without a loved one. During this period called *shiva*, meaning seven, the bereaved does nothing but sit around the house and eat from trays that are sent over from the neighborhood deli or brought by friends and family, and talk to people who drop by about what a great guy the deceased was.

All mirrors in the house are covered for the seven days. The reason for this custom has never been explained to me so that it makes any sense. It is a strangely comforting thing to do, but I think it would be just as comforting to cover your appliances. Rituals help. The more the better. They structure the first days, which are suddenly formless without the established boundaries of a long-term relationship, days when you have no knowledge of where your grief will take you. Rituals free you from worrying about what to do next. It's all there in the script. Enter left, wash hands with cup . . . cross down stage right, put *shmate* on mirror . . . cross left, light candle . . . sit center. For me, *shiva* was a transition period between the shock of dying and what I would find to be the shock of living.

After the funeral we drove back to my house. We washed our hands before entering, symbolically cleansing our bodies and our spirits. As soon as I got in, I lit a candle that would burn for seven days. The flame flickered and crackled with life. My father brought out some hard-boiled eggs that he said I should eat as a reaffirmation of my acceptance of fate and of the cyclical nature of existence. I washed down the egg with a beer. Endless trays of food, bowls of fruit, boxes of candy, and bottles of wine followed, accompanied by crowds of friends passing through.

The kids sat together at first, looking lost in their own house. But as people spoke to them and they found themselves able to respond, they loosened up, dropped in on conversations and talked with old friends. Miles talked about camp and about the play in which he had the lead. Seth talked about sports and how he had once kept his father company jogging around the golf course. "He couldn't believe it when I made it," he said proudly.

Asher played doorman. "Robert Liss died," he told everyone who entered. "Are you sad?"

I think it made them feel less vulnerable to be surrounded by so many adults who were interested in what they felt and who seemed to care about them. The house was full of food and packed with friends fussing over us. It wasn't so hard. Life was going on and we were being carried along with it.

Fewer people came by the second day. The kids went back to camp, my sister and father went back to St. Louis. I began to wonder what I would eat when all the food ran out. I worried about Bob's book and wondered if I would have to return the advance, which I had already spent. The mortgage was due, the bills were piling up like bat shit on my desk, and I was beginning to panic.

The third day was worse. Nobody came by. The lettuce on the food trays had wilted. My mother had run out of closets to clean and just sat around, looking tired and depressed. I felt forgotten, alone, destitute, and incredibly tired.

When Bob was in the hospital my energy had been boundless. I had a part-time drafting job until two in the afternoon. From there I went to the hospital until six. Then I went home to feed the kids, was back at the hospital by eight and stayed until he went to sleep. This went on for three months, and during that time I didn't know if the kids ever took a bath or what time they went to bed. But I didn't run out of steam until after he died, and then I couldn't seem to get enough rest. My mother said that I was catching up. I think I was hiding.

I could stay awake only for company. If someone came by to visit I was able to pull myself out of the daze that had settled on me like smog. I needed the stimulation of my friends to keep me going, but their concern and availability tapered off after the first days. They had jobs, they had families, and I guess they thought I was okay.

By the fourth day I was spending more time in bed than out. I was on tilt. There is an Arab custom that directs someone who is beset with problems to go to sleep for a few days. The idea is that when he wakes up, the problem is often resolved. Mine wasn't.

On the fifth day I went to see Bob's doctor whom we had both trusted throughout the ordeal. I needed to talk to someone about Bob's death and remembered that he had invited me to come and see him after things had settled down. I knew that he would listen and maybe even be able to help me. There were two things on my mind. I felt terribly guilty about having slept in my bed at home while Bob died alone in the hospital. But what gnawed at me more than that was my inability to face the absolute pointlessness of his death.

I waited in the chair next to his secretary's desk and stared out the window at the dismal skyline made up of elevated expressway ramps. After about ten minutes she led me into his office. He sat behind a desk crowded with books and papers. Bob's file had probably already been closed out. After a year and a half of notes, observations, attempts, and hope, the bottom line was "deceased."

"You know," I began, "I feel awful that I wasn't there with Bob when he died. After all we went through together it really bothers me that he had to die alone. I guess I should have stayed there that night, but it had gone on so long and he kept hanging in there and I needed to rest and see Asher. But I really think I made a mistake and I should have stayed."

"Death isn't like it is in the movies, where you die in someone's arms and are aware of that last moment," he said. "That rarely happens. Bob was okay at two in the morning when they checked him. At four he wasn't breathing. If you had been there you wouldn't have noticed anything until they tried to revive him. So you shouldn't feel bad about not being there."

"Well, I have another thought on my mind." I paused, took a deep breath and continued. "I wonder if you learned anything from Bob's case. Will you be able to treat the next person better because of what Bob went through?"

I was grasping vainly for some purpose for all Bob's suffering and for all the difficulties that I knew were to come. I felt that if something had been learned, his death would make some sense and be easier to take. If someone someday could benefit, then that would make Bob into a kind of hero who had died in action and not a victim of our ignorance. I had been hanging on to an illusion, and I wanted something to help me maintain an edge on that hold.

"No," he said, "it was such an unusual presentation of the disease. No, I didn't learn anything."

Not anything? Couldn't he have lied? I toppled off the edge.

4

On the sixth day I broke *shiva* and went back to my part-time job. By the seventh day my mother had gone back to St. Louis with Asher, and for the first time in my life I was alone. Everyone expected me to be terribly upset when I found myself finally alone.

"Please sleep with my mother, because I'm going away," Asher begged my friends. "She'll be lonely." This got a few embarrassed grins from the guys, but that didn't deter Asher. He was worried and kept right on soliciting for me.

My mother was worried too. "Why don't you come back to St. Louis with me?" she asked. "I hate to leave you all alone."

My friends were also anxious. "Look," one said, "if you feel too bad alone, just call or come over. I'm never in bed before two in the morning, so if things get rough, you don't have to be alone."

As I drove my mother and Asher to the airport, I too began to worry. Anxiety is contagious. I wondered if I was doing the right thing. I had no idea what it would be like to be absolutely alone. Maybe it would be a disaster. Maybe it would be a relief. Maybe it would just be boring. But I knew that this was the first step necessary in setting my course as a single person. If I couldn't make peace with being alone, I would have an enemy for life.

I had never been alone before, at least not for very long. Not for a period of time that I couldn't see the end of. I was the second of six children, so there was always someone around to bounce off. There was always someone ahead of me to try to keep up with or somebody behind me to try to get away from. There was always someone to bug me, someone to pick on, someone to take care of, someone to hug.

When I was ten we moved from La Salle, Illinois, to St. Louis. As we drove out of town that last time, I said good-bye to every familiar building I could make out in the pre-dawn darkness.

"Good-bye, La Salle Theatre. Good-bye, Kaskaskia Hotel. Good-bye, Fredman Brothers furniture store. Good-bye, Talking Bridge."

I bounced up and down with excitement in the backseat of our car, clutching the purse my best friend had given me as a going-away present. The magical darkness of the morning was broken as the sun began to rise. It appeared suddenly and steadily spread itself over the endless cornfields of southern Illinois. The fields stood barren in the December cold and, as I looked out at the landscape, I felt chilled and alone.

The lone Buick on Route 66 was speeding southward, taking me from one house to another, from one school to another, from one best friend to another. I was sitting in the backseat between two of my brothers, whom I hated because they pulled legs off grasshoppers and stepped on ants, but I snuggled up to them anyway, glad that they were there, and fell asleep.

Eight years later I went off to college, leaving my family and my pack of friends. I was alone for the time it took me to fly from St. Louis to Boston. For two and a half hours I was suspended above my life, cruising at 30,000 feet and every bit as high on the excitement of leaving home. I looked down through the clouds as the Midwest was left miraculously behind and the landscape turned mountainous. I cheered when I caught sight of the free expanse of ocean and the city on its edge that I felt was my oasis after eighteen years of wandering in the cultural desert of the Midwest.

God, I made it, I thought. Those fools have let me leave and I'll never go back. God, this is so neat!

I didn't have to worry about a thing, because when I landed I would not be obliged to find a job or make connections with people or chart a course of action. All that had been taken care of by my father, who for $5,000 a year had hired Brandeis University as a support system to feed me, educate me, and supply me with friends. My only obligation for his generosity was to pass all my courses and find a husband.

I met Bob at Brandeis during my sophomore year. The leaves were just beginning to turn when we fell in love, and we were married the next year before the summer was over. For the next two years we ate together, slept together, took courses together, and protested together. After we graduated and bummed around Europe, Bob got his first full-time job and I was alone with eight hours every day to fill up as I chose. I had three kids in the next three years.

That was the extent of my experience with being alone when I put my mother and Asher on their flight to St. Louis a week after the funeral. On the way back to the house, I found myself hoping that I would be so shocked by the feeling of being alone that I would freak out and get it over with. I thought that grief was something you could pass like a kidney stone. I was anxious to get into it, to feel really alone and awful, to feel anything besides "I don't know" and "I can't" and "what'll I do."

I used to have a recurring nightmare in which I would be trying to get away from some adversary. The harder I tried to run, the heavier my legs became, until I was almost totally immobilized with what seemed like cement hardening in my veins. This was how I saw myself responding to Bob's death, and I didn't want to shuffle through another day. I wanted something to happen. I wanted to get going.

When I pulled the sheet off the mirror in the front hallway, I saw my reflection for the first time since Bob had died. I was oddly unchanged. My tan had faded in the last week, but other than that there was no perceptible difference between the wife and the widow. I had expected the events of the week to bring on some obvious and dramatic change, but they had not in themselves really changed me. The change would occur only when I began to act in my new role and others around me reacted to what I did. I was in the eye of the storm, waiting for the condition of the wind to pick up and define me.

I went up to my room, disappointed by the lack of trauma. I lay down, closed my eyes and tried not to think about the past. This was a mistake because the past was sad but it was known. The alternative tenses were impossible, and panic began to avalanche.

The kids would have to be fed. . . . What would I do? My part-time job supported the metal in their mouths but nothing more.

The house would have to be maintained. . . . What would

I do? Paint was peeling in the stairwell and I was afraid of heights.

The book was unfinished and the advance was spent. . . . I couldn't write. I could barely even tell a story because I always rushed for the punch line.

The kids were approaching puberty. . . . What would that mean? What would I tell them? How would I explain sex to them? How would I show them how to tie a tie? I couldn't even untie one.

Who would sail the boat? I was afraid of flipping over . . . my knuckles turned white when I held the tiller.

I had been the bionic woman for the year and a half since Bob's illness had been diagnosed. I had managed to graduate cum laude with a degree in architecture. I had taken care of the boys, the house, and Bob when he needed it. Why suddenly was I floundering? Why was I feeling so helpless and so incompetent and why was I so incapable of action?

And what about fun, I thought, how will I have any fun? And movies—who will go to movies with me and who will I cook for and who will I go shopping with? Who will tell me I can splurge on something crazy? Who will urge me on? Who will enjoy me? Who will applaud?

I pulled myself up from the bed and from the luxury of self-pity. My feeling of insurmountable helplessness was beginning to scare me, and I forced myself downstairs to act out my first day alone.

I started by cleaning the house. It was still immaculate from my mother's visit but I cleaned the clean. Then I listened to my favorite cuts from all my records. I skipped meals and just grazed standing up at the refrigerator. I peed in every toilet. I fed the dog, watered the plants, and waxed the car. I rearranged the books. I made a drink. I cried. It was two in the afternoon and I wanted to get into the car and go to visit Bob as I had done every day at two o'clock for the past three months. But he wouldn't be there. Another dying soul would be in his bed and another frightened family would be waiting for a last-minute change in plot, hating the ordeal, wishing it were over, dreading its being over.

And although I hated the hospital, hated the nurses, hated the interns, and especially hated the parking lot attendant, I suddenly missed them all and missed the way my day had been orchestrated around them. And even though Bob had been sick and it was awful to see him, I missed those visits and our relationship regardless of how sad it had become. My mirror was gone, and without that reflection I had no clear image of myself.

Bastard, son of a bitch, shithead. I cried, not really knowing if I were cursing Bob or God or myself. I called Cynthia, trying to drum up some definition.

"Cynthia," I said, "I'm talking to myself."

"Bonnie, I'm glad you called. The Twenty-Four Collection is having a sale. I'll pick you up in five minutes."

The Twenty-Four Collection always has an odd mixture of clothes and art. I could never decide whether you were supposed to wear an item or get it framed. I don't remember what I got or what I did with what I got. I do remember telling Cynthia the story of my last visit to the store. I had been there with Bob, two years before, when I was looking for a dress to wear to my brother's wedding.

"I kept trying on these thousand-dollar dresses and parading in front of Bob and the kids. They were propped up on Turkish pillows outside the dressing room. The more expensive the dresses became, the faster they refilled Bob's wineglass. He was getting crocked and the boys were pigging out on jelly beans, and then Asher looked the saleslady square in the eye and said, 'I just cut a fart.' That was the end of that. The wineglass was snatched away and the jelly beans disappeared. I guess they knew that we didn't have the right stuff."

Cynthia laughed at the story and I felt a little strange. How could I be joking? How could I be shopping at this ridiculously expensive store? How could I make it through the day, through the week, through life? I was taking the first shaky steps. One step, another, call a friend, clean a file, organize Bob's newspaper clips, read some poetry, pay the bills, watch the tube. And when it's finally a reasonable time to go to sleep, go upstairs to bed.

I felt empty and dull and not very real. I didn't even feel anxious about being alone. I slept until ten the next morning and woke up only because the phone was ringing.

"Hi. Good morning. How was it your first night alone? Are you all right?" It was my mother.

"Yeah, I'm fine."

"Did you sleep okay?" she asked. "You know, I was thinking maybe it was a mistake to take Asher back with me. Maybe you shouldn't be alone now."

"No, I'm okay," I said. "I want to be alone for a while, really."

"Are you sure? I could send him back or you could come to St. Louis if you feel lonely."

"No, I'm okay."

"Did you have trouble sleeping?"

"No, really."

"I'll call Friday. If it's too hard alone, call us or come in."

"Okay, bye."

Alone was not the problem. Alone was okay. The problem was something much more piercing than alone, and if you are influenced by everyone's expectations of what should bother a suddenly single person you will always blame your problems on being alone. And with this scapegoat you may never be able to put your finger on what it really is that's so difficult, and it will remain with you undefined.

The real problem is balance. When someone you love and have lived with for a long time leaves, you lose more than company. Half your personality, the left-hand limit to your behavior, is gone. You are bereft of your own definition.

What had been my definition?

For most of my adult life I had fit myself into a role: I was the thesis to my husband's antithesis. Reacting that way to each other, we had made our way through a sea of events. And the synthesis of our combined selves was this—he was the sail and I was the keel. After he died I was in trouble, because the keel keeps you from slipping off course, but the sail gives you movement, and it's essential for both to work together if you want to make any progress. It took me a long time to understand this metaphor, which explained so much of my initial inability to make decisions and to act—so much of my ambivalence.

We don't realize how much of what we do is a reaction to the personality of our partner. Without that body on the other side of the seesaw you can't get off the ground or balance the board. When your partner is gone there is no way that your accustomed behavior makes sense. So a death means more than the loss of one of the pair. It means the passing of the other as well.

5

Of the many emotions that bombarded me right after Bob died, probably the most notorious were anger and guilt. Anger has a definite purpose. It is a productive emotion— you get mad . . . you act. And even if that action involves nothing more than kicking the dog or breaking some dishes or yelling at the kids, that can be enough sometimes. Anger has done its job. It has gotten you off your ass and moving.

Guilt, on the other hand, is unproductive and sets up hurdles along the track. But no matter how careful you are to ward it off—no matter if you see a shrink or try est or smoke dope until your IQ and age match in number—guilt will find you. It will slip in through your defenses and seek some unprotected spot in your psyche, and, claiming squatter's rights, it will make a home there.

I was no exception. Guilt had found me. It had squeezed its way in and was doing what it could to trip me up. My friends and relatives had been extremely supportive. After Bob died they did everything to prevent the intrusion of guilt into my already shaky perception of the situation. They coddled me.

"You did everything right," one said. "Bob was lucky to have somebody so great to stand by him."

"You were perfect," said another.

But I knew I hadn't been. I had made mistakes. I had rarely taken the kids to the hospital for visits. Bob said that he didn't want to see them until he got better. I was always worried about their transmitting some infection, and I thought his condition would scare them and his fading would leave them with a haunting memory. So I tried to protect him and them and their memories and felt that I had done the right thing until Asher told my brother Jerry, "My father died because I didn't visit him enough." With that, I knew I had made a mistake.

When I found out that Bob was sick, I didn't quit school to spend every moment with him. I took a full load, graduated, and then got a part-time job so that I would be in a position to take over if I had to. This choice was to some degree a mistake because the studying affected our evenings together and the job kept me from the hospital for part of the day.

Although Bob's doctor had said I needn't feel bad about not being with Bob the night he died and that there had been no real moment of death, I couldn't help feeling that he was wrong about that. I should have been there. I left because I was tired and figured I would see him in the morning, and that had turned out to be a mistake.

Everyone kept telling me that I was wonderful and perfect and special, and all the while my mistakes sat unnoticed and unweighed and metastasized in their seclusion. It would have been so much better if someone had said, "You weren't so great. In fact, you were really a shitty wife. You didn't spend all your time with him. You really let him down.

You were a slob with your kids too, by the way. They're a real mess now."

And then my old pal anger would have come to my aid, and I imagined yelling back, "You're wrong, you know. Bob was glad that I went back to school and learned a profession. I mean, he knew that I was on my way up shit's creek, but he didn't have to worry about that so much because I was getting myself a Goddamn paddle. And I was there every day and I gave blood when he needed it and I saw that he had a private room and private nurses when he needed them. Sure the kids are upset and confused because he died. That's natural, and they're adjusting. So don't give me any crap."

In defending myself I would have confronted my own doubts and sense of guilt and I would have won the debate because my mistakes had been minor. If I had had the chance to argue, I could have convinced myself of that. I could have worked it out. But nobody told me I was anything less than perfect, and the guilt sat and waited until Thanksgiving, until I was beginning to regain my stride, to throw a hurdle in my path.

Every Thanksgiving my mother puts together a big family reunion in St. Louis. She begins planning in September, eking out commitments from each of us. By October, she has worked herself into a frenzy of arrangements.

"Does Danny sleep upstairs or in the basement with the grandchildren? Does Bonnie get her old bedroom or should Jerry and his wife Carol get it? If Eileen is seated next to Irwin or Debbie, will there be a crisis before or after soup? Should the children sit together or be separated? Is the stainless adequate or should the silver be polished? Melamine or Wedgwood?"

By the third week of November, everything is worked out. As each of us arrives, she greets us at the door and assigns bedrooms as we enter. The table has been set for two days and there are place cards on each plate.

I didn't want to go home for the Thanksgiving festivities that year. When I went to the airport Wednesday afternoon, I thought about putting my kids on a flight to St. Louis and getting on the next plane to anywhere. I wasn't eager to see my family.

A few weeks before, my son Asher had asked, "Why did you marry Bob Liss? He died. Why did you marry him?"

I told him that I loved Bob and that nobody knows when somebody is going to die. But his question cut through my veneer of reason. In some crazy way I felt that by marrying someone who died young, I had let everybody down—my brothers and sisters, who looked up to me, my kids, my parents—and I didn't want them to see me.

As we waited for our names to be called for the standby seats, the options open to me went marching through my mind, and I knew none would work. If I go, I'll regret it. If I don't go, I'll regret it. If I both go and don't go, I'll regret it.

"Will standby passenger Liss, party of four, please check in at the gate," the agent announced.

I took the boarding passes and the third option—I both went and was never really there. I spent the entire holiday incognito. Nobody saw me. Nobody but Asher. I was hiding behind my new clothes and my newly bleached hair. My brother Jerry met us at the airport. He gave me a solicitous hug.

"How's everything?" he asked sadly.

"Oh, great!" I said. "My job is terrific. I've been flying absolutely everywhere. And the housekeeper is terrific too. The place is cleaner than it's ever been. I haven't seen a roach in months. Mom won't know what to do with herself when she comes down to visit."

"But how are you doing? I mean, really." He was uncomfortable with my good humor.

"Oh, I feel great. I'm screwing a twenty-nine-year-old dermatologist," I lied.

He looked embarrassed and checked to make sure the kids were out of hearing range. They had rushed ahead up the concourse. "Well, uh, great," he said. "I mean, is it serious?"

"Oh, God, no," I said happily.

"Well, great. I mean, you look great." He finally smiled. We hugged again and, following the kids, went out to find the car.

At the Thanksgiving meal, I was a wall without a flaw in my black Basile blouse and skirt, drinking Russian vodka on the rocks. I jabbered about my job, the kids, my life, without any hint of sadness.

"The job is great. The housekeeper is wonderful. The kids are terrific. I finished the book and my editor thinks it's really going to do well. They want me to promote it on television."

Everyone was staring at me, waiting for me to crack, to start slobbering into my vodka and begging for the sympathy that they were prepared to give. They had expected grief and depression and were getting Doris Day. I had put up a carefully structured facade, like an architect who designs a funeral home with colonial columns and lintels to disguise what happens inside. It almost worked. I was so slick I nearly slid off my seat when Asher got up, marched around the dining room table to where I was sitting and asked, "Are you guilty?"

I was too shocked to respond.

"Guilty of what?" my sister Eileen asked, as Asher wandered back to his chair and we all returned to our pumpkin pie. The question went unanswered.

But that night I had a dream.

I was at work, and a murder had been committed or maybe it was just a death, but I assumed there was foul play involved because my colleagues were wrapping up parts of the body in tinfoil and sticking the small packages in the flat file with the architectural drawings.

I took it upon myself to find a better way to dispose of the body. I realized that it would decompose in the flat file and smell up the tracings. Pretty soon someone would notice the packages, open one and, after discovering the contents, assume there had been a murder committed just as I had, even though I didn't really know for sure what had caused the death.

So I took out the packages, loaded them into the basket on my bike and pedaled off, looking for a bonfire to throw them into. I came upon a group of kids building a fire and asked them if I could throw in some spoiled meat. They said okay, so I threw the tinfoil packages into the flames and left.

When I was back at the office I realized that if the fire went out, somebody could discover the packages, open one, and see that it did not really contain spoiled meat as I had claimed, but a decomposing part of a human body. If they found the kids who built the fire, they would get my description, find me, and link me to a murder that I had nothing to do with and that may not have occurred.

I hired a private plane and a pilot to fly me back so I could check out the tinfoil packages and make certain that they had burned up properly. They hadn't. The fire had gone out and the kids had left. I started the fire again and prepared to leave so that I wouldn't be associated with the increasingly sordid situation.

The plane was there but the pilot had disappeared. I looked around frantically for him, and a sleazy-looking guy with a mustache appeared and offered to fly me back. After an incredibly shaky takeoff, the sleazy guy admitted that he had never flown before and then he landed short of the airfield on the expressway.

I was sure that the police would notice us in no time. They would wonder why I was flying with a creep who had landed an airplane on the highway and why I was leaving a bonfire filled with tinfoil-wrapped packages of decomposing human parts. I knew that I would be linked to the murder of a person who may very well have died of natural causes.

My dream had answered Asher's question. No matter how irrational it is, we do feel a deep sense of guilt after the death of someone we love. It is the guilt that comes from an extended association with death. It is the guilt of surviving. It is the guilt we carry for the thousand little wrong choices that we made along the way. It is the sudden chill that can surprise you as you are biting into a peach or watching a rainbow slice through the clouds.

Anger is one of the few emotions that helps us pull through a period of grief. If we are lucky, our anger will find a focus and transform into action and creativity.

Initially my anger about Bob's death focused on his unfinished manuscript. I was angry that the book was incomplete and that I was left with the hassle. But I was really outraged by what it symbolized. The writing had faded in direct proportion to the writer. It had started off as a strong and vital record of a man's perception of his life and then slipped into a string of disconnected thoughts and sloppy perceptions. The progress of his disease could have been traced more accurately by the quality of his writing than by the results of any of the thousands of tests the doctors demanded for gathering information.

It drove me crazy. Every time I read the manuscript I grew more and more furious. It staggered, it failed, it absolutely flat-assed died. I knew that there was nothing I could do about the fact that *he* had died, but there was something I could do about the book, and in a way that satisfied my anger. It made me feel as though I were adjusting fate. I was determined to work out an ending to the book so that it wouldn't piddle out as he had. I had never written anything before, but I had no doubt about my ability to finish the work, not with anger running tackle for me. Before Bob died I told him not to worry about the book. I told him I would see that it got finished.

"Don't make the sentences too long," was all he said.

After he died, when I actually sat down to write, I became totally involved in the project. Nothing could come between me and the object of my anger, not my kids and not the job. I locked myself in my room at night with the manuscript, with the irrational fury and strength of the Hulk. My mother was worried about my obsessive behavior and thought I should give it up and get a ghost writer. I told her that I thought a ghost writer in this case would be morbid and that it wouldn't save time. I was writing as fast as I could think, which was faster than I could talk. I blamed my persever- ance on the money that was involved.

"I spent the advance, Mom. I have to fulfill the contract or return the money."

"Listen to me, your father will give you the money if you have to return it," she said.

I didn't want to listen. The truth was that I had under- taken the writing project for myself and not for the editor. I was writing because my anger needed something to wrap itself around. I was writing to eat up any free time I might have had to deal with. I was writing because the family was used to a writer, because the house was used to the pecking of typewriter keys. I felt a little like a transvestite as I sat in Bob's chair and peck-pecked at his machine. I even used paper with the *Miami Herald* masthead for the rough draft. If my mother hadn't given away Bob's clothes after he died, I probably would have put them on to work in. I was nuts but I was productive. The anger gave me energy.

I wrote twelve pages. I kept the sentences short. I wrote about myself and about Bob's illness. I found some unfinished pages that Bob had been working on, pieced them together and ended the whole thing with my sailing nervously but optimistically into the future. At the end of August I made an appointment with his editor in New York. I wanted to deliver the work in person. I told her there was a lot that needed to be discussed and worked out between us, but really I just couldn't bear to cut the cord and put the manuscript into the mail.

Neither Bob nor I had ever met his editor. She was the only one who bid on the book when Bob's agent put his proposal on the literary market.

"Everybody's afraid you'll die before you finish the story," she said when she called Bob to introduce herself.

"Oh, don't worry, I feel fine," Bob had said. That was back in December, when he was running three miles a day and still working at the *Herald*. "And anyway, if I die, Bonnie will finish it."

After two months I had what I thought would be a passable manuscript. But the night before the trip to New York I was filled with doubt and couldn't sleep. I read and reread the story, which grew increasingly dull as the night wore on. By the middle of the night I wondered who would really give a shit.

In the morning I put Bob's manuscript and my twelve pages into a shopping bag and went to the airport, feeling insecure and foolish about the whole thing. But once I got on the plane and into the air I was all right. I was always all right at 30,000 feet. My shopping bag was tucked snugly under the seat in front of me and a stranger was in the seat next to me, quietly reading the *Wall Street Journal*. Looking down at the familiar coastline of south Florida, I relaxed for the first time in months.

I've found that if my mood is right, if the person next to

me is innocuous, if there is no turbulence, no movie, and no elaborate meal service, the time spent traveling on an airplane can be a real gift. It is the gift of feeling absolutely removed from the situation below, absolutely between places and events, absolutely free.

I had lunch with my friend Soozy in New York, took a bus from 30th Street up Madison Avenue to 56th Street, and got off to walk the rest of the way uptown toward the Eighties, where Bob's editor lived. As I paused to look at some shoes, I caught my reflection in the store's window. My dress was wrinkled, my hair had long outgrown the limits of the cut, and my shoes were falling apart. What I saw reflected in the storefront was a bag lady with her whole life in the shopping bag she was dragging up the streets of New York, without direction, without much of anything but her memories and her shopping bag. I rushed into the store and bought an expensive pair of shoes in an attempt to camouflage that image. Then I quickened my pace as I approached 82nd Street, a bag lady in new shoes.

The sun managed to slip around the buildings and find the pavement. Summer was everywhere. It was in the blue sky that seemed low enough to hold on to the tops of the buildings. It was in the ever-escalating humidity and in the heat that was escaping from the sidewalks. Summer was on sale in the shops along Madison Avenue.

The bag lady made it to the editor's building and tapped on the security door rather than ringing the bell, with a lightness that said she did not feel she should be there. She was a little surprised when the elevator man greeted her politely and took her up to the third floor.

The apartment was filled with cats, books, and the smell of coffee. I put down my bag, had some coffee and delivered my pitch.

"Look," I said, "this manuscript is really incomplete. I wrote something to try to finish the story. I know that Bob wanted to end the book with a positive tone, but he didn't have time. His writing just kind of piddled out. You'll probably want to cut the last sequence, which doesn't make any sense and would be really depressing. But maybe you can do something with it. I don't know. You don't have to use what I wrote. I guess I could get a ghost writer. I wasn't sure what to do, so I just wrote something, but it's probably shitty. At first I thought it was okay, but I reread it last night and I think it sounds pretty dumb." Great pitch, kiddo.

"Let me read it," she said. "Bob trusted your instincts and so do I. We have time. We're ahead of schedule, so I'll read it and think about what we should do and let you know. Don't worry about what Bob wrote. That's my job. I have a good feeling about this book. Did he have a title?"

"Well, nothing was specified in his notes. I called it *Fading Rainbow*."

"I like it."

When I left her building I walked over to Fifth Avenue to take a bus downtown to where I was staying. I began to cry after the first block. My project was complete. The object of my anger wasn't with me anymore. It was being scrutinized by an editor who lived on 82nd Street, and I wasn't sure what would motivate me anymore. I would go back to Soozy's apartment and we could go shopping at Macy's or go to a movie, but there was nothing I had to take care of. The void was oppressive. I had been debagged.

"What happened?" asked Soozy when I walked in. "You look like shit. Was she horrible?"

"No, Sooz, she was fine. I guess I have postpartum depression or something."

She laughed and poured me some wine. We sat and talked until the wine and the closeness of someone who knew me well got me past the wave of sadness. Then we went back outside to enjoy the rest of the day.

The editor called me in Miami a few weeks later. "It's

good. I liked it," she said. "It's a powerful story but I want you to write more."

"I said all I had to say."

"Look, there are places throughout the book where the reader will ask questions. Bob would have gone back and filled in those gaps. But he can't, so you'll have to do it for him in an afterword. People will want to know things like how you met and why you went to Israel and why you came back. Chronology, the book needs chronology. I'll write you a letter and list all the areas that I think need to be expanded. If you can give me about forty pages by late November, we'll make the publication date that's been scheduled."

What the editor wanted sounded simple enough except that I couldn't seem to recall anything of our relationship before the illness. All the images I had of our life together were shaded by the last three months of Bob's dying. I had not been able to see beyond the fading. My memories smelled of death.

Her letter arrived at the end of September. It contained an outline of topics she felt I should cover in my "afterword to Bob's book." So it *was* a book. It had graduated from a manuscript to a book, from a pile of papers to something that would be reproduced and bound and sold and read.

"Please call when you get this if you need to talk more," she wrote after she had completed her list. "Otherwise, forge ahead and good luck. You can write."

I had a coach. I was preparing for a major event and I had a coach. I sat down with her list of exercises and her pep talk and my typewriter, and I began the first workout.

1. Your marriage

—when/where/how

—your background and Bob's/your families

We met at Brandeis so long ago, when he wrote poetry and smoked a pipe and could make me laugh and was a little shy and young and healthy.

I wrote about how we first met, about how I said, "Pretend you know me," to a stranger and squeezed in next to him in the crowded student coffeehouse, trying to avoid someone else. I wrote about how we fell in love in the backseat of a car with the Beatles blaring on the radio.

2. *Israel*
—*why*
—*your life there*
—*the reason for the return to the U.S.*

We went because we had all those kids and didn't want to settle down. Our parents thought we were nuts and we laughed at them and went anyway because we were young and wanted an adventure and because we were nuts.

I wrote about our life on the collective and about how we left after a year and bought our own small farm. I wrote about the kids and mainly about Asher, who was not developing within the range of "normal." Asher didn't speak. He made noises like a fifties cartoon character called Gerald McBoing Boing, but he would not speak. And then I wrote about closing the chapter on our youth and going back to America to work out the problems that develop eventually in any relationship.

3. *Florida*
—*your new life*
—*Asher's problem from your point of view*
—*your decision to go back to school*

We went to Florida because it was warm and because we had found out after five years in Israel that winter was an option we no longer wanted. Florida, the tropical paradox, where the further south we went, the more north it became. Until we hit Key West, the last stop before you fall off America and land, anticlimactically, in only three inches of lukewarm ocean.

I wrote about Asher and about adjusting our expectations

to accept his problem. I wrote about learning to yield. I wrote about going back to school and studying architecture and how that affected my relationship with Bob. I thought about the bad times and the good times and picked out stories to share that would communicate the ever-changing balance of the two.

As I wrote, I was struck by the reality of my life with Bob and by the realization that years I had spent with him still existed for me. Nothing could touch them or take them away. My recollections of the past and our life together were comforting and not at all depressing.

There is a tendency to avoid evoking memories after someone dies. At first I stayed away from favorite spots. I didn't trust myself in places we had enjoyed together. I thought they would remind me of my loss and be upsetting. Friends politely dropped Bob's name from stories. There was an unspoken agreement not to look back. But this total avoidance of the past did not protect me from anything. It actually made things worse because it reinforced the irrational feeling I had that my whole life was pointless now because Bob had died.

When I finally found myself led to a favorite haunt by a friend who did not know my old hangouts, I was amazed at how good it felt to be there. And when people stopped by to visit, it was the very conversations about Bob that left me with a feeling of well-being. It was important for me to understand that death hadn't wiped out my past. It had changed my future, but it had not nullified the past.

As I wrote, my memories unfolded like a tissue-paper flower opening in the water. I was no longer motivated by anger. My purpose was to narrate a situation and a loss. I was not out to alter fate—only to describe it so that it would make sense. As my thoughts expanded, the awful shroud of the immediate past and present lifted. I could remember when things were different, when death was not the lead character in our drama together. By the first of November I had forty pages, and the sad memories had taken their place among all the others.

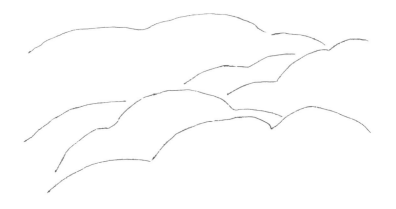

PART TWO

7

We take over in little ways. We warm up to it as playfully as a kitten stalking a ball in preparation for a rat.

I hated to run, I hated it because it was in style and because it made my side ache and my tits bounce. Bob used to run three miles a day while I disdainfully stayed at home and did "something productive" like mix a drink. And one day, before he took his final turn for the worse, I ran with him around the golf course. I walked more than I ran; Bob slowed down for me and we did the three miles together.

After that I went with him every day, and every day I could run a little more and he could run a little less, and one day he couldn't run at all. I ran alone. I went the full three miles every day for him until he had to go into the hospital, and then I stopped running. I never ran again.

The running had been an experiment in taking over. It was practice in the resolve and stamina I knew I was going to need. It was also a kind of sympathetic magic.

During each of my pregnancies, Bob had put on weight before I did in anticipation of the experience that he could not have. Husbands that belong to a particular tribe in Africa go into labor along with their wives, moaning with pain that is not really theirs. Sympathetic magic is an attempt to share an experience with someone you love, partly so it does not become a wedge between you and partly as some primitive attempt to fool the gods.

"Listen to this, God," the African says, in effect. "Someone is suffering for the birth already, so let her be."

"Okay, God," Bob was saying, "I put on weight, so spare her a few stretch marks."

So, every afternoon, while Bob sat on the porch popping vitamin pills, I put on my tennis shoes and walked down the block to the golf course, crossed the street, and began to run.

Hey, God, I said to myself, the Liss is still out here running. The Liss is strong and well and not really dying. Ha, I passed the pond . . . I'm gonna make it to the big tree. God, just let me make it to the big tree . . . made it . . . now, the drinking fountain . . . just let me make it to the drinking fountain . . . keep going, legs . . . five more steps . . . oh, yeah, the drinking fountain. See that, God?

It was March. The days were warm and dry for Florida. The air was healthy. The prevailing wind coming in from the southeast blew all the imperfections of the city out over the Everglades, leaving the sky absolutely blue. I walked from the drinking fountain to the cluster of tall Australian pines and then began to run again.

I think Bob felt better about things when he saw me running. We never discussed it, but he kept track of my pace, asked which landmarks I had reached, and gave me hints on how to run further. He knew he was on the way out. His concern about my ability to fill the eventual void in the family wasn't verbalized, but I knew it was there. He talked about it obliquely, leaving me pieces of the puzzle I would eventually have to put together.

"Start off slowly," he advised, "pick landmarks that you are sure you can reach, and go for them one at a time. Pick a course you feel comfortable with and think you can almost finish. Pace yourself. Walk if you have to. Don't worry about your speed or about looking good. Just go the distance. Later on, when you get stronger, you can refine your form and build up to a formidable pace."

The future at that point seemed to be something I wouldn't be able to handle. But running had been a controlled experiment for me to learn to go the distance, and I saw it as a metaphor for the distance I had to go to develop new skills and to make progress in a world I couldn't even imagine.

I was an economic illiterate at the time of the death. I had never worked for a full day's wages in my life. The bills came in and I paid them every month with someone else's earnings. The only mathematical function that existed as far as I was concerned was subtraction. I never needed to work, and at thirty-five I wasn't sure if I was capable of doing it. But Bob's death had left me with a primitive fear about my survival, and this fear helped to cancel out my feeling of insecurity.

Will I have enough to eat? I worried. Will I be able to feed the kids when they get back from camp? Will the orthodontist repossess the metal in their mouths? Should I drown the dog to save on Alpo? Was I eligible for food stamps? Could I learn to do addition?

I had nightmares about roof leaks and rotten plumbing and storms blowing down the walls of my house. I had fantasies of wealthy men falling for me and taking me and the kids from our crumbling house on Prairie Avenue to a fancy solid home on Sunset Island with a freezer filled with steaks and lamb chops and a live-in maid. The economic picture of the surviving Liss family was sinking from bleak to a surreal mixture of anxiety and fantasy.

"Start off slowly, pick landmarks you are sure you can reach, and go for them one at a time."

The house was not in order. We needed a wage earner, and I knew that my first step in reestablishing order would have to be economic. I had to find a full-time job so I could afford to buy groceries and keep my house from crumbling further, and so I would have medical and dental insurance benefits. But having a full-time job also meant that I would have to show up in the same spot five days a week at eight-thirty in the morning and make it through the day, past two, past three, all the way to five. It meant I had to be responsible, agreeable, and, most important of all, I had to be concerned with success.

I have always been a highly motivated learner. But it was the process of becoming and not the actual goal that had motivated and excited me. My pattern had been to pursue something complex and demanding, master it, and then switch my course of study. After I got my degree in architecture, which came after a degree in fine arts, I thought about going to medical school.

"What do you really want to be?" my father asked.

"Well," I said, "I guess if I keep it up, I'll be the best-educated corpse ever to be buried in Dade County."

I could have been described graciously as "intellectually curious," but a more accurate observation was that I suffered from an underlying fear of failure. If you never do anything, you can never really fail. If you are forever becoming, then you are always on the brink and excused from any kind of judgment.

My economic paranoia pushed me over the brink. No one was out there working for us. My part-time income was small change. The fear of being judged harshly at a task paled next to my fear of poverty. I remembered that when I was about ten years old my parents went through a difficult period in their marriage. I used to listen to them fighting in the kitchen, which was separated from my room by four inches of drywall, insulation, and some cheerful vinyl wall covering. I felt helpless and vulnerable when they fought.

"That's it. I've had enough of this crap," my father yelled one night. "I'm going to California."

Then a door slammed and a car pulled out of the garage. Its tires squealed a good-bye. I lay in bed awake the rest of the night, worrying about how we would survive without a father who went to work every day to bring home groceries every night. We'd probably have to eat at Rexall's, I thought.

And then the next morning he was there, drinking coffee and doing the crossword puzzle as usual before he went to work.

"How was California?" I asked.

He laughed, but I didn't. The specter of destitution was still haunting me—the six of us lined up on drugstore stools washing down our cold grilled cheese sandwiches with the scant water held in the cone-shaped paper cups.

The first "landmark" I had to reach was economic security. To feed and house my family, I had to get a full-time job and develop an attitude about myself that would allow me a chance at success. This was a landmark I was sure I could reach. If I could get an A in calculus after twelve years without a math course, counting on my fingers because I couldn't remember how to multiply and didn't trust my calculator, I could certainly hold a job. It was up to me to watch out for the hurdles that I placed in my own path to success —to steer clear of them at first and then knock a few over and finally stop putting them there at all.

The next decision was which job to go after, because whatever I chose would start me off in a direction that would define my future.

"Pick a course you feel comfortable with and think you can almost finish. Pace yourself."

I decided to stay with the airline where I was working part time, and requested a drafting job in the Facilities Department. I preferred this to a more conventional position with an architectural firm because of my financial situation and my familiarity with the airline company. The typical architecture graduate is treated like a medical intern in his first job, which comes complete with long hours, minimal pay, and repetitive tasks. At twenty-two, one can afford that, but I was thirty-five and couldn't.

The airline paid better than an architecture firm and provided the benefits I needed with a dependent family. My experience working there had been a good one. As a part-timer I worked with the Corporate Design group, which consisted of one architect, one interior consultant, and me. The architect and interior consultant planned the special-service clubs and wrote standards for the design of all offices and public facilities for the company. I put in my two cents on everything and then drew up the concepts that developed.

After Bob died and I returned to work, I found that my job was a lifesaver. It gave me somewhere to go every day and some graspable problems to work on. I felt more at home there than I did at home, where there were so many traumatic adjustments to make. My job was a familiar course and I felt comfortable with it. I could pace myself with more confidence there with friends to support and encourage me than I could have at a new, unfamiliar office. The last thing I needed at that point was another change in my life.

I got one anyway. I had had a wonderful boss in Corporate Design. Even though I was a part-timer, I had a real sense of working with him and of being challenged. When I began to work full time in the Facilities Department, it wasn't the same, not at first. I had been used to a creative working environment and had to gear down to the monotony of drafting.

"Walk if you have to. Don't worry about your speed or looking good. Just go the distance."

I went the distance. I came in every morning at eight-thirty and made it through until five. In the morning the senior draftsman assigned projects and miscellaneous errands for me for the day, which I always finished by noon. After that I was on my own because he wouldn't assign me any more work. He liked to keep a healthy backup so we would always look busy and overworked. I hated to sit around, so I drummed up some action for myself by going to the individual project architects and engineers and asking if they needed any drafting. Most of them didn't have the time to draft for themselves or the patience to wait for the drafting team to get around to doing their work, so they'd slip me a city ticket office or a cargo building or a holdroom.

Then I was asked to file. I lasted a month.

After that first month I had no doubt about my ability to handle a full-time job, but I didn't know if I wanted to. The pace was too slow and I was bored. I needed work that would utilize my talents, and filing was not one of them. I had to keep singing the alphabet song just to remember the correct order.

One of the engineers knew I was unhappy with the drafting situation and told me that Bill Griffith, his manager, was interviewing to fill an opening for a project architect.

"Why don't you apply for it, Bonnie? You can do it. If I can do this job anyone can. I'll recommend you to the Grif if you want."

I wasn't sure if the job was for me. It would mean more exciting work, more money, and a chance to learn an advanceable career. It would also mean travel, long hours, and being away from home. Any man of the family would go for it. I began to realize that that was precisely what I was becoming.

I spent a few hours in front of an open file thinking it over. I wasn't worried about the additional responsibility the job would demand. I wasn't worried about the long hours or the travel. What bothered me about the job was that it would change my role and I didn't know how that would affect my family. If I got the job, I would have to get a housekeeper to cover for me when I was out of town and to do a lot of the domestic tasks even when I was there. This would mean that I would lose part of my identity as the mother. If I got the job, I would have to work harder and with more aggression, and I would begin to take on characteristics that we are all used to assigning to the father's identity.

Bob had a trick for keeping me in my place. He didn't invent it; what he would say I had heard long before our marriage. "Boys with aggressive mothers," he would tell me when I had the philosophical advantage in an argument, "grow up to be faggots."

That had always stopped me dead. I succumbed. I had been hearing that line for so long I believed him. I believed society. If I hired a woman to do what I had done, if I gave up some of my identity as their mother to fill the more aggressive role left by their father, the boys might be left with confused feelings about their own sexuality. But if I didn't go for the job, would I be able to file construction documents and do bootleg drafting for the next thirty years? Was it worth hanging in there to insure that my kids would have enough to eat, straight teeth, and heterosexual tendencies?

Somewhere between the Rs and the Ss I made my decision. I would kick away the hurdle and go for the job. The Grif might not even hire me, and if he did, the worst thing that could happen would be that I'd never have a daughter-in-law.

"Later on, when you get stronger, you can refine your form and build up to a formidable pace."

I waited until no one was watching and poked my head into Griffith's office.

"Bill, do you have a minute? I'd like to talk to you."

"Sure, come in," he said.

"I hear that you're looking for an architect," I began.

"Bonnie," he said, "shut the door. I don't want to start the secretaries gossiping before we even begin a discussion."

I shut the door. They started gossiping immediately. Doors to managers' offices are shut for only two reasons. Either the manager is telling a gross joke or he's discussing a change in someone's status. The minute the door shut everyone knew what I was up to. Bill Griffith wasn't one to tell gross jokes to a woman.

"I wouldn't have any trouble working with you. But you should think about it. This job will mean being away from your family one or two nights a week. I'll try to give you stations that you can get back from at night, but there'll be times when you can't. Will that be a problem?"

"No. It won't be a problem. I'll get a housekeeper."

"Okay, I want you to give it some time. Think about it. This position will mean a real change in your life, but it's a great opportunity. On Monday, if you still want it, the job is yours."

I was elated when I left the office. I wanted to walk back in and do it again. I wanted to say yes right away and start before I. M. Pei showed up and applied for the position. When I got home, I tried to explain the situation to the kids.

"Boys, sit down and listen. There's something I want to ask you. I have a chance to get a better job, but it will mean that I have to travel and be away sometimes in the evenings or in the mornings, and maybe even all night. The work will be more fun for me, but I'll have to get a live-in maid to take care of you when I'm not around. Do you think I should take it?"

"If it's more money, take it," advised Seth, the pragmatist.

Miles sat sullenly and finally let it out. "The only thing that bothers me about your taking the job is that it's dangerous."

"Dangerous?" I asked. "How is it dangerous?"

"Well, you'll be flying a lot. What if the plane crashes and you die? What happens to us?"

"Listen, I have a will. It's in the file cabinet. If anything happens to me, all you kids would go to live in Albuquerque with Jerry and Carol. But planes don't crash as often as you think. It's just that when they do, the accident makes the news, so you're really aware of it. Actually, I'm more likely to be in an accident on my way to the plane than on the plane itself. I don't think the possibility of a plane crash is a real danger, Miles. In fact, the only real danger I can see with this job and with spending so many hours sitting on airplanes is the danger of getting hemorrhoids."

"Okay, you can take the job," he said.

"If you get a foxy maid," added Asher.

I did both.

8

I love the smell of kerosene in the morning. To me it smells like progress. I would catch the first whiff as I turned off the Airport Expressway onto LeJeune Road and the jets screamed in for landing, pouring the last vapors of fuel into the air above me. I could smell it all the way to the parking lot where I rolled past the sleepy guard in the morning darkness and parked my car. It grew stronger as I rode the employee bus across the ramp under the wings of the planes waiting to be serviced, loaded, pushed back, and tugged out to the runway. There, unseen by a still sleeping city, encased in two hundred tons of polished aluminum, I would once again have the chance to defy the laws of gravity and tradition and prove that a woman could fly.

From Miami I always flew north over the long flat state that sticks out from North America like a sore thumb. Beyond Florida, the airline industry divided the country into three geographic regions. To get to anywhere in the first region, I had to go to Atlanta and turn right. To get to anywhere in the second region, I had to go to Atlanta and turn left. The third region was New York, and I could fly there directly. The aircraft barreled down the runway. I sat within, uncertain, and peered out the window, waiting for the moment when we would lift off the ground. The sun cracked the horizon. We were off. We rose steadily over the streets that were still lit by the high-intensity crime lights, and over the clouds that were menacing the coast with a morning storm, and only when we leveled out at our cruising altitude of 30,000 feet did I relax. It was as though we had reached a scenic turnoff at the edge of a vast plateau, where I could sit and feel safe and look out to where I had been and to where I was going.

I had begun the process of breaking into the fraternity of professional men. For my initiation I had to learn a technical vocabulary and cultivate an interest in football. For dues I had to give up the luxury of being able to act like a dumb broad whenever I felt lazy. In return I got the chance to develop into a resourceful person.

There were three other guys in Bill's group. Jim Stewart was the senior project architect and the second in command. When the Grif was out of the office, the Stew ran the show. Walter ("Dixie") was a project engineer who handled most of the southern stations because, as the Grif explained, "he speaks their language." Michael Nulty, known as "Mick," was the senior project engineer. He was a veteran, having been with the company longer than anybody else. Dixie began calling me "Bliss," and it stuck.

The group ran like a neurotic family, which helped me feel at home. The Grif would start off the day getting coffee with the Stew. Then the two would schmooze for an hour in Bill's office while Dixie sulked in his cubicle.

"He hates me," Dixie moaned every morning. "He's always in there talking to the Stew. He hates me."

"Aw, who gives a shit," said Mick, who was already buried in his drawings.

"Look, Dixie, why don't you just walk over for coffee with them, tag along into Bill's office, and shoot the shit too. What's the big deal?"

"I don't drink coffee. Coffee isn't good for you. Be good to your body, Bliss, and your body will be good to you." As he spoke he peered around the corner. "They're still in there. I think they're in love. He hates me."

The coffee excuse didn't make sense. He could have substituted a soda or a carton of milk and joined the morning schmooze session. I kept offering solutions that were chucked unreasonably until I realized why I was so hung up on his exclusion. He wasn't. He probably wouldn't have joined Bill and Jim if they had sent out for a round of Yoo-hoos. The social structure of our design team had been established well before my entry. Everyone knew his place, and although there was the usual ritual bitching and moaning from time to time, they were all comfortable with the arrangement that had evolved.

I was the one who had a problem to work out. My concern for Walter was misplaced. It was I who had to find a way to fit into the group and determine the quality of the fit. I was the one who had to demonstrate whether I'd be seen in the group as the woman who knew her stuff or as the one with the bumps in front.

At first I tried to keep out of everyone's way and not ask too many dumb questions. I thought if I could just avoid looking stupid, all the guys would think I knew what I was doing. And technically I did know what I was doing. As a project architect I was responsible for any facility work in the cities Bill assigned me. When a project was requested, I had to determine the scope of the work, draw up the design, and write an estimate. Once the design was approved and the funds were allocated, I had to see that the work was done according to the specifications I had written, within a reasonable time, and within the budget.

But the technical know-how was only a small part of the picture. Probably 80 percent of any job is form. This is the kind of know-how that you don't learn at school, so it is easy to appear stupid and confused when you begin to work. If I could have taken a course in the etiquette of my particular niche in the working world, I would have memorized enough bullshit to ace the class. But there was no course. The only way to learn the vocabulary and the techniques for getting things done, the only way to learn to make small talk without looking small, the only way to know how much you can bluff and push before someone blows the whistle and yells "foul," is to start doing it.

The first thing I had to learn was the vocabulary. Vocabulary is a barrier professionals use to maintain their mystique. It is the series of passwords that turn an office into a fraternity. Without the vocabulary you are ignorant, and even if you know your stuff you can't perform. At first I couldn't decipher the instructions I received.

"Hey, Bliss, I need an FCE for a three-position ATO in IND with three CRTs. I need it right away, so see if you can pull an AFM before five."

How could you die and leave me in this mess, I thought, blaming Bob and fighting back tears. I can't do anything. I don't even know what he wants me to do. Why didn't you warn me about this?

And then I remembered how Bob had struggled with the vocabulary of the medical journals just to be able to understand what was happening to his own body. "It's all very simple," he told me. "Once you learn the language it's all obvious. I'm dying, and they don't know shit."

I translated Bill Griffith's request with Mick Nulty's help, and by four that afternoon I had finished the Facilities Construction Estimate (FCE) for an Airport Ticket Office (ATO) to operate with three computers (CRTs) in Indianapolis (IND). I spent the next hour trying to figure out what an

AFM was so I could "pull" one. I searched through the standard practice manual to find a description of the AFM form. It didn't seem to exist.

At five I went into Bill's office, handed him my estimate, tried to bluff my way through. "Here's the FCE you needed, but I didn't have time to pull the AFM. Can it wait until tomorrow?"

"Well, don't worry about it." He glanced through the FCE and added with a laugh, "Unbeknownst to you, Bliss, you have pulled your first AFM. Thanks."

I went back to my desk and stopped Walter before he left for the day. "What's an AFM, Dixie? I feel like an idiot. I just pulled one and I don't even know what it is."

"You pulled an AFM. Golly, Bliss, that's terrific. When they make you a vice-president, just remember who your friends were. After one month they have her pulling AFMs! Hey, talk about women's lib. You *have* come a long way, Bliss, and I knew you when you were just pushing a pencil. The Grif must like you. I didn't get to pull an AFM for a year. He really likes you."

"Come on, Dixie, is it some kind of permit or computer cable?"

"No. So you don't know what AFM stands for?" He paused to pick up the one folder on his immaculate desk and pop it into his file box. He slipped on his blazer, ripped the day off his calendar and shot it into the wastebasket, pronouncing it "over." He said, "It stands for 'another fucking miracle.' Stick with me, Bliss, and you'll learn the technical terminology in no time."

The flight attendants passed through the cabin and began the meal service. I discreetly refrained from wolfing down the parsley and the lettuce that decorated the fruit salad. I stoically saved my croissant for the second cup of coffee. I had mastered the art of eating leisurely and politely on an airplane and no longer finished before the passenger next to me unfolded his napkin. I had even stopped chewing up my chicken bones and accepting every drink that was offered, but lunches in the Miami office were still a problem.

When I wasn't traveling I had lunch with the guys in the employee cafeteria. Besides eating with the Olympic speed and the obsessive thoroughness of a chronic mother, my presence put a definite damper on small talk. But after a few months they began to ignore me and their conversation returned to the old recipe of business and football, spiced with a little profanity and a touch of gossip.

I didn't add much. I wasn't familiar enough with the politics of our department and I had never been to a football game. Up to that time my luncheon dialogue had been confined to "finish your milk" and "don't play with your food." Since neither was particularly appropriate in the employee cafeteria, I just ate and listened until finally I felt bold enough to join in.

"I saw *North Dallas Forty*," I offered, thinking this would interest someone since it was about football. "It was good."

The balding, graying heads were all bent over their food trays. Nobody seemed to be listening.

"I liked it a lot." The lack of interest made me nervous, but instead of shutting up, I began to babble. "I think I may even go to a football game this season. What a bunch of characters. But, you know, I was really disappointed in Nick Nolte's body."

Everyone looked up and stared at me.

Oh, shit, I thought, what did I say now. Shit, I should have kept my mouth shut. Is it criminal to criticize a football movie? Is Nick Nolte a Facilities folk hero? Is this kind of like criticizing John Wayne or Frank Sinatra or the Pope?

Nobody said anything. I looked from face to face and got the same frozen stare. Finally Dixie broke the ice.

"Bliss," he said, "when did you ever see Mick Nulty's body?"

Everyone hooted with laughter. I blushed and laughed too, but only for a moment. I noticed that they were a little too comfortable when they could laugh at me, a little too eager for a slipup. I knew that I had to be very careful and very correct if I was going to move into this neighborhood and fit in and actually belong. I was the first black on the block.

I peered out the window and could see a city sprawling along the Florida coast. The sea defined the state on three sides, the descent to Atlanta defined the fourth. When I got to Atlanta I would have to turn right and go to Greenville to check on the progress of the departure lounge expansion. The week before I had gone to Atlanta and turned left for Indianapolis.

Before I went to work for the airline, I had had two ways of evaluating a city—walk it or ride it. Each way of experiencing a place gave me a different set of events, sounds, and smells to react to and left me with a different perception of exactly where I was. One was slow and direct. The other was fast and enclosed within the limitations of the street and the vehicle. Now I had a third method—fly it.

Indianapolis has no character from the sky. There are no man-made or geographic landmarks to distinguish it from any other small city. Every house below me had a pitched roof with gray asphalt shingles. Every fifteenth house had an aboveground swimming pool. A huge racetrack was tossed nonchalantly into the landscape.

All I could perceive as I flew into Indianapolis was lack of planning, grayness, and ever-expanding growth. The city seemed to be a malignancy on the broad back of the Midwest.

Besides processing arrivals and departures, one of the functions of an airport is to welcome and orient the traveler. This can be done with graphics, with girls in grass skirts, with beggars, or with a military guard, but it is most impressively done with the visual presentation of the place itself. Most airports fail to do this because they are built outside the center of activity and cannot take advantage of the city's scope to tell you where you are.

I was there because my FCE had come back with an EA —an Expense Authorization—and a notice to proceed with the construction of a new ticket counter at the ATO in IND. I had ten hours to do it. Once an ATO opens it cannot be closed unless service to that city is terminated. Every day tickets must be sold, boarding passes distributed and planes loaded. It cannot be closed for remodeling. Any ticket counter work has to be done in phases or during the inactive hours of the night.

The last flight left Indianapolis at 9:00 in the evening and the first one the following morning was scheduled for a 7:15 departure. That meant I had ten hours to rip out the old counters, computers, ticket printers and miscellaneous inserts and install the new ones. By 6:00 A.M. the counter had to be ready to operate. The agents had to be able to sell tickets and the computers had to be "up" and spitting out information.

Tyler came to Indianapolis with me. He was a computer technician and was there to put the computers back in place and make sure they were running properly. He was tall, muscular, sported a tie and a mustache and looked infinitely more in charge than I did. I was the conductor and Tyler was the one who had to go "bing" on the triangle at the right moment, but when a problem arose the workmen involved in the project would ask him the questions. He was the man, so he ought to know. When he tried to direct them to me he couldn't, because I was off getting coffee for everyone.

I didn't feel comfortable as an authority. I could easily and graciously give men coffee but not commands. Tyler had enough common sense to figure out what needed to be done, but that was not his responsibility. While I was hiding out behind the implied role of a female, he was forced to do my job. Tyler could have filed a civil liberties suit. It was a clear case of sexual harassment.

By 10:30 we had all the counters ripped out. The carpenters, who had been due with the new counters at 10:00, hadn't appeared. We cleaned up, pulled cables, drank coffee, and waited. I called the carpenter shop at 11:00 but there was no answer.

At 11:30 I was beginning to think that they might never show up. Perhaps they had been in an accident and our counters were at that very moment being ground to pulp on the highway. Perhaps they had gotten stoned and taken off for Terre Haute or Bloomington or wherever it is you take off for when you live in Indianapolis.

"Tyler," I said, "what if they don't show? What'll we do?"

"If they don't show, *you're* in a heap of trouble. There won't be anywhere to sell tickets from in the morning."

The terminal was empty except for us. It was cold and overlit and looked like the set for a sadomasochistic movie. The last flights had gone and Indianapolis had gone to sleep. We had six hours left.

"Even if they show, we'll never get it done."

He laughed. "What do you mean, 'we'? They'll come and *you'll* get it done. Don't worry. You worry too much."

At midnight three very strung-out carpenters arrived, looking as if they had been up for days and were fading fast. The counters were incomplete and covered with glue where the laminate had been hastily applied. One counter slipped and crashed to the ground as they unloaded it from the truck. I looked around for Tyler to give me some help. He was trying to find the cables that went down to the ramp-level operations office.

"Hey, Tyler, I'll go get you some more coffee if you keep an eye on the carpenters."

"Look, Bonnie, you're in charge. Everyone's asking me what all to do next, and I'm just here to make sure the computers work. I don't know what needs to be done."

"I'm sorry. You're right, but I don't really know either."

"Well, you'll have to learn quick 'cause you have only five hours left to make it happen."

I used to nag Bob to cut the grass every Sunday, and it occurred to me that it would have taken much less energy to just cut the grass myself. But so much of our relationship was based on his doing things and my getting him to do things that doing the job myself seemed like mutiny. And now the yard was a jungle and the grass went untended, but the grass was one thing and the ticket counter in Indianapolis was another. I had to get it done and since I couldn't find a guy to badger into managing it for me, I would have to evaluate the situation and find a way to get the job completed on time.

I tried to encourage the carpenters to work faster. I explained how important it was that the counters be in by 6:00 A.M. so all their fellow Hoosiers could be boarded efficiently onto the morning flight to Atlanta. That drew a blank stare. I chastised them for being late, careless, sloppy, and completely unprofessional. That drew a hostile stare. Then I took a can of acetone out of their workbench and began cleaning the glue off the surfaces of the counters.

"You don't have to do that, lady," one said.

"I know I don't. But it means a lot to me to get the job done and I don't see how you can finish everything by 6:00."

They began to work alongside me. They hadn't had time

to make the face of the counter so we removed the fronts from the old units and tacked them on. At 5:30 the counters were set and the equipment was in place. Tyler punched the code into the relocated computers and we held our breaths until the green letters began marching across the screen in response.

"We're alive," he said.

At 6:00 A.M. the passengers lined up and were processed for their trip to Atlanta.

The plane veered to the west. Clouds covered the landscape below us, but we were way above the clouds and the morning sky was blue and undisturbed. Even the violence of the jet-driven carrier could not touch the blueness. There is something eternally neutral about the color of the sky at 30,000 feet. It is a pure cool wall to hang my pictures on.

I saw myself at a party the director had given at his house over the weekend. One of the Facilities managers was retiring. There were drinks and snacks and small talk. I had gone alone. After the second round of drinks the group rearranged itself and I found myself standing next to the manager's wife.

"And whose wife are you?" she asked.

My friends froze in helpless anticipation of the impact of her words.

"I'm nobody's wife," I said. "I'm one of the guys."

9

"You're a damn fool," my grandfather used to tell me when I was in high school, "and you don't have any sense. Why aren't you religious like your brother? You're a beatnik and an atheist and a damn fool."

In his eyes, the girl was irreligious, irreverent, and wild, and this image stuck despite the fact that she had grown to be a pretty normal woman doing the normal "reverent" things. A year after our marriage, Bob and I drove across the country and stopped in St. Louis to visit everyone.

"So, how do you like married life?" my grandfather asked.

"Fine, it's great."

"So, you have to admit, God was right about something." He spoke emphatically, as if he were making a point in a debate, as if I had been arguing with him.

"Yes," I said with a laugh, "he was sure right about that."

"Yeah," Bob added as we walked out to the car, "if God meant for us to live alone, he wouldn't have bothered to vary the plumbing."

I had no argument with marriage, and after we had kids it made even more sense to me that we lived in committed pairs. I could barely manage to take care of the family with a husband. I wondered how single parents managed to stay afloat. And then I found out. You learn to tread water against the tide. You struggle, you sink, you fuck up. As I tried so hard to rebalance the family so it could operate without a marriage, that elusive and magical "balance" turned out to be only something you wave to in passing. The winds are variable and so is the course, and when you think you have really balanced things, you have only stopped paying attention to them.

Bob was the husband and I was the wife. The balance between us fluctuated with our perception of ideas or events. Sometimes we were in accord and sometimes we fought and the fights were great because they taught me something new about the details and the intensity of how I felt. We kept up our running dialogue throughout our marriage—for better or for worse, in sickness and in health.

"Well, I'm the boss," Bob said, trying to end one argument.

"Oh, yeah," I said, "well, so what. I'm the biss."

Husband versus wife, boss versus biss, thesis versus antithesis, and the occasional moment of balance. And when there was only the wife, the running dialogue stopped. It was all monologue. I had to make the decisions alone, and instead of facing an argument when I was heading toward a dumb move, I found myself facing a mistake.

"What do you do with your babies when you travel?" I was asked solicitously in the middle of a departmental negotiation.

I was winning a point and the woman (of course) who asked the question was getting in her last jab. It is very easy to make a working mother feel bad. Punch her below the belt and watch her squirm.

"I don't have babies," I replied, "and when I went to work I got a housekeeper."

It sounded simple—I got a housekeeper when I went to work. But there was nothing simple about finding a suitable person to fit into our family. The history of our housekeepers is the story of all the confusion and ambiguity I felt as I set about being the "momdad." I tried everything. I tried normal, I tried bizarre, and nothing worked. We hadn't really accepted the situation, so it was impossible to accept the fix. When I went to work I filled the economic void but left a base open. I had only one prerequisite in mind to guide me in the essential task of hiring someone to cover the bases, to referee, and to maintain the ground rules. I had to have someone who would agree to take the job.

Why was I so careless? Part of the reason was that I wasn't ready to let go of my identity as the housewife. If whoever blew in did a shitty job, so much the better. That would just prove how essential and correct my fourteen-year choice to be a wife and mother had been. I was also worried that any serious prerequisites would frighten off applicants. We were hard-core. My kids were unhappy, my house was a mess, and I was frantic. We bore no resemblance to the Brady Bunch. But the real problem was my inability to define what I meant by "a suitable person." I had no one to bounce my ideas off of. There was no dialogue and I didn't explore the complicated question of what our family needed. I left it all to fate. Maybe God would be right about something else.

I called two agencies and waited for a nibble. Violet responded first. She was from Jamaica, she was young, and she agreed to take the job. I was elated and spent the weekend converting the TV room into her bedroom. I cleaned the closet, cleared the bookshelf, and set out linen for the bed.

Violet arrived on Monday as she had promised, and at first everything was wonderful.

I started to spend time with each of the boys. It had been months since I had paid any attention to them. I had been so caught up in Bob's illness that I didn't have time or energy to face the kids. With Violet doing the housework, I could help with their homework or take them for bike rides or just listen and watch as they played.

After I accustomed myself to working a full day and the kids settled into the school year, I began to notice the direction the household had taken. The cupboards were organized, the beds were made, the house was clean, and the occupants were miserable.

I had never had a maid before. I didn't realize that she would always be there. She was there when I got up and when I went to bed. She was there when I yelled at the kids or came home drunk. She was there when I was irrational and when I was depressed. I thought that anyone would do, but this was not the case. It is impossible to live with someone you don't trust. I didn't trust Violet. None of us did. She was honest and never took anything that wasn't hers, but this was not the kind of trust that turned out to be important. We didn't trust her with our weaknesses, and the strain of hiding them made us hostile.

There we were, four people in three thousand square feet of space, licking our wounds and trying to figure out how to make it through another day. Enter the fifth, who only wanted to earn a living and have some bucks to send to her family in Jamaica. Her presence made us feel invaded, and she wasn't prepared for the troops hiding in the trenches waiting to pounce.

After work I would come home and eat dinner with the kids. Then I would go up to my bedroom, they would go to theirs and Violet would go to hers. All the rooms were spotless. As I read or organized bills, the kids would do homework and fight with each other. Violet would watch television, shave her eyebrows, drink coffee with salt, and read magazines. The house was too clean and all the doors were closed.

None of us felt comfortable with each other. Violet had worked only for families with babies and disposable complications. She thought my boys were rude. My boys were used to baby-sitters who played cards with them and let them sneak down to watch a late show, and they thought Violet was a drag. There was a quality of disorder in my house that had evolved through the years. It was a fine patina on the surface of my surroundings. She destroyed it with a frown and a swipe of Lysol.

"You're trying to take Dad's place and she's trying to take your place," said Miles. "I don't like it. I don't like her and I don't feel at home anymore."

There were arguments and misunderstandings and insults on both sides. I hid in my room and never took a stand because I was afraid she would leave and I would have to find someone else. I pretended everything was okay so I wouldn't have to deal with it.

"You're upset because of Bob," I rationalized to Miles. "Anybody I had in here would be a red flag and would make you mad."

Asher refused to let her wait for the bus with him. "I'm a big boy and I'm not standing with her," he said.

Seth imitated her behind her back while his brothers giggled, leaving Violet hurt and angry.

"She throws away my homework," Seth complained. "She keeps the house too clean. Grandma won't have anything to do when she comes to visit. That's not fair."

Sometime between eleven in the evening and six the next morning, six months after she walked in with all her possessions stuffed into a shopping bag, Violet decided she had had enough of us. She disappeared in the middle of the night, leaving her clothes hanging neatly in the closet and her freshly shaved eyebrows forming a ring in the otherwise immaculate sink. The television was blaring and the side door was wide open.

I had to catch the 7:20 A.M. plane to Orlando. I got the kids up, gave Miles a list of when to do what, and rushed to the airport. I called before boarding my plane. Violet had not returned. Asher had caught his school bus, Miles and Seth were reading the funnies and in fifteen minutes would go out to catch the city bus to go to school. I was home by five that afternoon. Violet still had not surfaced. I began to worry that something might have happened to her, so I called her sister Sylvia.

"Violet's all right. She's not here now, but she's all right."

"Does she want this job?"

Silence.

"All her clothes are still here. Does she want her clothes?"

Silence.

"Look, Sylvia, I'll assume that your sister doesn't want the job anymore but still wants her clothes, and I'll hold them until she comes."

I was relieved that she was gone. The kids were delighted.

"We don't need a baby-sitter. We'll take care of Asher," said Seth. "She was mean. She cussed when you were gone. She called us 'fucking brats' and she hit Asher and called him a dummy. She made out with her boyfriend in the living room."

"Get Grandma," said Asher. "Grandpa won't mind."

"Get a maid who can cook," said Miles.

What I got was Pete.

In six months as an employer I had learned something. I learned that we needed more than someone who would take the job. We needed more than clean floors, organized shelves, and made-up beds. We needed a person we trusted and could include in our family. Nothing had made me feel lonelier than having someone in my house, in my life, with whom I could not communicate.

"What did you expect?" Walter said when I bitched to him about Violet. "What you need is a husband."

I had broken out of my mold. I had gotten a job and was doing it and liking it and paying my bills and feeding my kids. Walter was wrong. What I really needed was a wife.

I had met Pete some months before at a party. It was the first party I went to without Bob. I started to go, changed my mind, undressed, and then decided again to go. As I pulled on my clothes I tried to visualize how I would be, surrounded by merriment with a drink in hand. Friends would approach. They would be solicitous and kind and ask me depressing questions and I would give them the depressing answers with my second drink in hand. Then after I thoroughly depressed everyone, I'd go out to the garden with my third drink in one hand and my fourth drink in the other, sit under the palm trees, get totally bombed and talk to the ferns. There would be no one to scrape me off the wall and take me home, no one to tell me I had been amusing when I hadn't been, no one to gossip with over cognac before bed.

I arrived late and tried to squeeze through the groups of people to get into the kitchen, where I could hide and not feel as if I were a fog settling on the evening.

"Bonnie, good to see you. How are you doing?"

"Uh, okay, fine. Well, actually, shitty."

"Uh, well, nice to see you. We'll give you a call."

What else could I say? "Oh, terrific. I finally have enough closet space." Or "Great, he snored."

I made it to the kitchen. Stephanie slid off the counter and gave me a drink. "I'm glad you came," she said. "Now, here, get drunk and have fun or don't have fun but don't worry. You're terrific."

I drifted outdoors and was milling through the philodendrons, when a tall young man in jeans came up and introduced himself as Pete Ryan. "I was sorry to hear about your husband. He was one of the only people around the *Herald* who was encouraging about my writing."

"Oh, you write," I said.

"Yeah, free-lance for *Tropic*. I did the first-person piece on what it's like to be a straight ballet dancer."

We sat on the steps leading up to the pool and talked about Bob and about writing. The palm trees were silhouetted against the moonlit sky and swayed like black ghosts in the breeze.

"I'm leaving for Los Angeles in the morning," he said. He went to get me some more wine and was swallowed by a crowd. I suddenly felt alone and out of place, so I slipped out the garden gate, found my bike, and rode home. The moon brightened the road but not me. I felt tired, anesthetized ever so slightly by the wine and the memories, and had difficulty pedaling the flat, easy blocks to my house.

I'm getting old, I said to the night, old and dry and responsible and full of shit.

I ran into Pete again at a friend's house just after Violet left. He had come back from Los Angeles broke, unemployed, and anxious to move out of his parents' house. All I really knew about him was that he wasn't a queer ballet dancer. But I liked him and Bob had liked him and everyone seemed impressed with his writing. He was one of the gang and the gang was like family, and I felt certain the kids would benefit from having a guy around the house. So I cornered him and went straight to the point.

"Pete, I have a proposition to make to you," I said. He grinned, flashing dimples, and winked. "No, listen, I understand that you need a place to live. I need occasional baby-sitting. Say, one night a week, two mornings, one dinner. I'll give you free room and board if you take care of my kids while I'm traveling."

"Wow, really? Sure."

It was settled. Pete moved into Violet's room three days later with a duffle bag full of rumpled clothes, a large old-fashioned typewriter, a Labrador, and a hangover.

At first, the kids were confused. This guy looked like fun, but did he wash dishes, floors, and laundry? Pete was con-fused. They were smaller than he but what if they didn't listen to him? And what did I really want from him? Would *he* have to put out? I was confused. How would I be able to get this six-foot-three-inch budding drunken Irish writer to be comfortably responsible for three budding fatherless Jewish kids? Would *I* have to put out?

Asher broke the ice. "Peach, Peach," he asked, mispro-nouncing Pete's name, "are you the janitor?"

"No, I'm not the janitor. I'm the governess. No, I'm the governor. That's it, I'm Governor Peach. And this here is my dog Koala."

Seth examined Koala, who was drooling on the floor, and said, "I hope he doesn't bother Doobee. She's a Lhasa Apso and is real small. I hope he doesn't—you know—*bother* her."

"Don't worry. Koala's too old to bother anybody. He's about 120 years old and can't get it up anymore. He won't bother Doobee. He'll just think about it."

Pete grinned at me and winked. "Nice kids, Mrs. Liss."

As I left the room I heard him say, "And if you're good boys, I'll let you see my *Playboy* magazines."

They were good. We were all good. Peach was fun and we were starving for some fun. Everything had been so heavy and so serious—losing, mourning, changing—and it was good to finally hear some laughter. It was as if the cloud that had hung over our sad old house for so long had finally blown away. The neighborhood kids were back on the doorsteps looking for action. I hadn't noticed they were gone until they came back.

We began to feel like a family. We could all talk to each other and we tried to be amusing because there was someone around we wanted to amuse. The kids really enjoyed Peach. He played Frisbee with them, took them for walks, and wrestled with them on the living room floor. He listened to their problems. Miles had problems with girls, Seth had problems with school, and Asher had problems with just about everything. I was at work or traveling and Peach was home with the boys.

I enjoyed my work more because I didn't feel that I was deserting the kids. Peach was there. If I got home early I'd go to a movie with him or to a bar, or we'd stay up late, talking about writing. I enjoyed him as much as the kids did.

Of course, it got awkward. We were riding on the excitement of a new, unconventional friendship. I went to work and he stayed home with the kids. I thought it would work out because I was giving him a perfect chance to get some writing done. He had a place to sleep, food to eat, and seven hours a day of absolute quiet. He'd take out his typewriter when the kids left for school and he'd put it away when they came home. But he wouldn't, couldn't write. His writer's block was impenetrable. In the three months that he had his seven silent hours a day, the only thing he wrote was the first half-sheet of what he claimed would be a five-hundred-page epic on the history of dog washing.

He sulked around the house all day, not writing. And then it got bizarre. I came home from work one day and found a kid from up the block in Miles' room. He was tied up with sheets and gagged with a towel.

"He got too wild, Bonnie. I told him if he didn't stop running around and screaming in Spanish, I'd have to take action."

I let the boy loose and he laughed and ran around the house and out the door. "Listen, Pete, I don't think you should have tied him up."

"He liked it and he looked so funny."

"Well, I don't think his parents would exactly like it."

"Oh, who gives a shit. I told him if he said anything to his parents, I'd do it again and bring Koala up to lick his feet."

My parents were shocked when they came to visit me. My mother began cleaning the house the moment after she set down her suitcase. She gave Peach dirty looks whenever she passed the chair in the living room to which he had rooted himself with his pile of books, his porno magazines, and his Rolling Rock beer.

"I cleaned everything," she announced when I returned from work, "except that sink." She gave Peach the evil eye, led me into the dining room and continued in a lowered voice, "Bonnie, really, you've got to get rid of him. It doesn't look good. What if you go out on a date? What if a man comes to the house? How will it look? It won't look good, I'm telling you that. And the sink. Have you seen the sink in his room?"

"No, I haven't seen the sink, Mom. What's in the sink? Have Violet's eyebrows sprouted?"

"Bonnie, I think he's urinating in the sink. Listen to your mother. Get rid of him. It doesn't look good."

The honeymoon was over. We began to bicker. I complained about the dog digging holes in the yard and the mess in the house and the sink. My mother had been right. He was pissing in the sink. He sulked around the house and bitched about the bad mattress in his room, the mess in the house, and the heat.

I tried to be accommodating. I wanted him to stay "for the kids," but the more I acquiesced, the angrier I became. "If he thinks the house is a mess," I told my friend Cynthia, "he could damn well clean it up. I'm out there working, earning the money to buy food and pay the mortgage, while that asshole sits on his butt watching soap operas. He has no interest in himself, he's totally uncreative all day and then has the fucking nerve to take it out on me when I get home."

The Peach was turning into a pit. He was bored, boring, and bitchy. He reminded me of all the housewives I had known in Boston and of how we used to sit around together at the park or in someone's kitchen, drinking coffee or tea and watching our babies. I was married to a reporter, Jan was married to an engineer, and Barbara was married to a cab driver, but we had three things in common. We were all bored, boring, and bitchy.

Peach lasted three months. He went to his grandmother's for dinner one night and never came back. He took his dog but he left his clothes. I don't know why they always left their clothes. I could have opened a thrift shop.

I cleaned the house after he left. I disinfected the sink, I washed the floors, I beat the rugs until the place felt like it was mine again. The kids missed him and I did too, but it had gotten strange. Too many unspoken tensions and hostilities had found their way across the line of acceptable behavior.

"Get me another janitor," pleaded Asher, "who'll torture me and give me kidney shots."

At a neighborhood dinner party a few weeks after he left, Pete's name came up and I said, "I really don't understand why he peed in the sink. I guess it was just that he was so lazy. He had to take an extra step to get to the toilet."

"He was a pervert," said one woman, who wasn't too fond of Pete. "He was a pervert. That's why he peed in the sink. You should be glad he's gone."

And Stephanie, who had always been a fan of Pete's, said, "No, I think he used the sink because he's just so tall."

I put the next baby-sitter, a photographer named David, in my garage apartment. I thought a little separation would help, and it did. It helped him to deal drugs. I was the front for his flagrant and highly illegal side business/habit. I asked him to leave and he tried to talk me out of it, pleading innocence, guilt, remorse, anger, and, as a last resort, pathos. I held my ground and said no to him, finally taking a stand for what I felt was right for my family.

Bob would have thrown out Violet after a week. He would have given Peach a month, and David wouldn't even have had a chance to unload his crummy Pinto. But men are used to saying no. Women avoid issues. They get headaches, they get depressed, they get anything it takes to put off the actual no. I wore blinders so that when things got out of hand I wouldn't have to see. I wore blinders and turned to ice and waited until the problem went away by itself.

I began to understand why both Violet and Peach had left their clothes. They weren't sure what I wanted. Perhaps they thought I might come running after them, begging them to stay. "Oh, no, you read me wrong. I wasn't saying no. I was just being a jerk. Please don't go. I had my period."

And then they could come back and wouldn't have to bother unpacking. With David I was certain. I said no loud and clear, and a few extra times just to hear myself say it. He took his clothes when he left.

10

had been working as a facility architect for seven months when the manager of Corporate Design announced his plans to leave the company.

"Oh, God," I said when he told me the news. "How could you do this to me? I'll miss you so much. Whom will I talk to? Who'll laugh at my jokes? I want your job."

I wasn't the only one who wanted it. Corporate Design had its own little box near the top of the Facilities organizational chart. It was an independent niche between the regional managers and the manager of planning. You could tell it was a step up because the Corporate Design office had a door on it.

"It'll look good on my résumé," said a senior architect. "And it's the only promotion in town."

Unfamiliar with office politics and the chain-of-command protocol, I went directly to the vice-president of Facilities and told him I was interested in the job. "I like what I'm doing, but I think this would be a better chance for me to use all my skills, like my background in art," I said. And my background nagging a husband and kids, I thought. "Besides, I used to work in Corporate Design and I know what's involved."

I know how to harass vendors who've sold us crap, I thought, and peck at the guys downstairs in Facilities like a den mother. This may be the only job in Miami that I'm actually qualified for.

"I'm glad you like what you're doing," was all he said.

A few days later the Grif called me into his office and bawled me out. "If you were interested in the Corporate Design job you should have come to me and I'd have spoken for you. But, frankly, I don't think you're ready for it, Bliss. And I don't appreciate your going over my head and the VP doesn't appreciate it either."

But the Grif was wrong. The vice-president did appreciate it. He gave me the job, but there was a hitch.

"I have a problem," he explained. "The architects who deserve a promotion are deeply involved in completing the new Atlanta terminal. If I move one to Corporate Design I'll have to introduce someone new to the Atlanta project, and I don't think that is in the company's best interest. So I'd like you to manage Corporate Design until Atlanta is complete. At the end of the year, I'd like to review the position. Would you agree to take the job on an interim basis?"

I said yes. One year was a long time to ride a tide and I thought if I did it well enough I could keep the job.

"Well, at the end of the year don't expect me to take you back," said the Grif. "I thought you were interested in learning project management. That's why I hired you. So don't expect me to give you another chance at it."

"Aren't you nervous, Bonnie, aren't you scared?" one of the secretaries asked as I packed my desk for the move upstairs into my new office. The question surprised me, or rather my response surprised me. I wasn't scared at all. A few months earlier I had been afraid to open my mouth in the employee cafeteria, and there I was, moving to a highly visible position in the company, and I wasn't frightened.

What could they do to me if I screwed up? They could yell at me or they could fire me, but I wasn't nervous about that. Losing a job seemed little league compared with the other losses I had gotten past. There was nothing really important that they could take away from me.

I wasn't scared. I was fatalistic. So much had gone wrong. None of what I was doing was what I had planned. It all seemed to be out of my control, and this very feeling of not being in control of what I had always seen as my destiny— wife, mother, backseat driver—gave me my first sensation of freedom. I wasn't scared anymore. Being scared wouldn't matter.

What can they do? I thought. Let's get it straight. They can fire you, but they can't eat you. So what can really happen? Put my wad on number seven and spin the wheel.

In that spirit of bravado I flew to Puerto Rico on my first trip as acting manager of Corporate Design. My new position made me responsible for all the special-service clubs in the system, and I was going to San Juan because the club there was beneath all mention. I was as excited about the trip as a little girl on her first flight. I smiled at the guard in the parking lot. I shot the breeze with the bus driver as we crossed the ramp. I kidded around with the supervisor at the check-in position and was still smiling when the agent at the lift desk pulled the flight coupon off my pass.

Things were okay. I had a new baby-sitter, Sandy, who didn't curse at the kids or pee in the sink or deal drugs on the side. She was refreshingly normal, and I could leave home with a clear conscience.

The plane moved down the runway, bouncing gently on the stretch of asphalt that had been expanded and contracted by the alternate beating of the sun and the rain into a less than perfect surface. There was a sudden smell of kerosene, the rush down the runway, and the rush of that barely perceptible moment of lifting off.

Miami teemed with life below us. Its arteries were filled with the morning traffic that moved steadily into the heart of the city. The cars chugged along like tiny corpuscles on their continuous working journey as I was lifted higher into the open sky on my own peculiar journey to work. We flew over Brickell Avenue and over Key Biscayne and then we were over the ocean, rising steadily, setting a course that would take us over the Bahamas, over the Turks and Caicos islands, and finally into Puerto Rico. And when we got there I would be expected to solve design problems that had developed in a space I had never seen.

I looked out the window. There seemed to be no horizon. The water was blue and so was the sky. Only an occasional puff of cloud disturbed their communion. I could barely perceive the slim distinction between the sea and the air. Or was there really any distinction at all? It was like the difference between fear and excitement that is nothing but the attitude, the view of the viewer. What had changed in me in the past few months? It was not my ability, not my intelligence. What had changed was my perception. I was far enough away from the death not to be gun shy, not to be waiting for that tap of fate on my shoulder, not to expect that "act of God" referred to in the fine print of our contract. But I was still close enough to feel one thing—"what the hell."

I could see the sails of some boats below me, white specks floating across a cool blue surface. The first decision I made after Bob died was to sell our boat. He had been the sailor and I had been the hysterical woman aboard, otherwise known as the crew. But when a buyer showed up, I changed my mind and couldn't sell it.

"I want to learn to handle the boat," I told Henry. "Can you teach me?" Henry was over seventy years old. He had taught Bob to sail, and he probably had taught half of Dade County to sail. He was delighted that I had taken an interest in the boat.

I was nervous at first. I was afraid that if I touched the tiller something awful would happen. I was sure that if I took the tiller we would turn over and I would bump my head and drown or swallow water and choke or tread water and attract sharks. I was sure that if I took the tiller, I would not get back to the dock alive. So every time we went out I would insist on being the crew and make Henry sail the boat. One day he pushed me off the dock alone. I cursed and pleaded and then—what else could I do?—I grabbed the tiller, found the wind, and sailed off and came back. Nothing awful happened, so I did it again. I was shaking when I got back to the dock but it was not from fear. I was shaking with the excitement of finding out I could do something new. I was shitty at it—I pinched, I spilled wind, I came about when I should have jibbed—but it didn't matter. I had stepped out and seen myself as a person with a different kind of control, with the ability to perform. And it didn't matter that this perception was a product of my fatalism and of Henry's shove. It was a first step in the right direction.

We passed over Bimini. I spent a week there three years back, scrambling after kids by day and sneaking down from the room with Bob by night to drink in the bar where we were staying. One evening we sat next to a couple with a young boy, and when the man left to take the child upstairs, the woman leaned toward us and said, "He is not my husband. I have two other lovers, and my son, he is always asking, "Mama, how do you do it? How can you have three?" And I tell him, "I am the bionic woman." And then she got up to dance with the stranger who had been eyeing her across the bar.

"What an idiot," I said to Bob. "She thinks she's juggling three men and they're really juggling her. One day they'll dump her and she'll be alone with her kid wondering what happened." I savored a securer-than-thou feeling as I watched her dance.

And now, as I flew over Bimini years later, alone with three kids, I remembered the woman. I wondered if she were still dancing. As it turned out, I certainly hadn't had any more security in my life than she had had. I hadn't been able to control my fate by playing by the rules. I had been dumped into aloneness probably a lot sooner than she had. And now there was only today and getting to San Juan and what the hell.

The island of Bimini slipped under the left wing of the L-1011. We passed Eleuthera and San Salvador. Framed by my window, the islands became abstract shapes in an ever-changing composition of hot coral and cool blue. And then there were two blues below, the cold blue of the ocean and the warm Caribbean blue that is as innocent as hope. I wanted to dive into the inviting innocence of that blue.

We flew into a squall, and when we came out of it Puerto Rico lay below. We skirted the north side of the island, flying over the small towns and farms, over the refineries and factories, over Sears and J. C. Penney and Banco Popular, over shacks with rusted rooftops, over the monolithic brown condos of the almost rich, and we descended.

The terminal in San Juan is open to the air, but has none of the qualities possible in an open-air space. It is dark, confining, and confusing. Paddle fans hang over the ticket counters, moving the reluctant, humid aid through the dingy hall. Every flight seems late even if it is on time.

I found the club lounge. It was awful. It had a pink-and-turquoise carpet, overstuffed tweed chairs, blue love seats, and marble coffee tables. The lamps looked like Manuelian columns wearing top hats. The regional director came in and introduced himself.

"What do you think?" he asked.

"What do I think? I think it looks like a whorehouse that was popular in the fifties."

He laughed, agreed, and asked what I planned to do. As I outlined my plan for refurbishing the club on an extremely limited budget, I felt certain that I was making the right choices. I knew what needed to be done and I told him without my usual "ers," "ums," or nail-bitten "maybes." I was there to do a job, after all, and there was nobody around for me to lean on. There was no Tyler, there was no Henry.

I told the regional director what I could do to make the club look decent and what it would cost, and he told me to do it. Then I was off and running. I looked at the ticket counter, the holdrooms, the baggage claim area, and worked out design solutions for various problems. What was exciting about the day was that it went so smoothly. Everyone behaved as if I knew my stuff.

Can't they see through me? I thought. Can't they see through the facile corporate blah-blah to the terrified me who just wants to go home and read and paint and putter around the house?

But how could they? That me wasn't even there anymore. She had moved out. The new occupant was working and making decisions and excited about it, and this is what everyone saw and responded to. I felt good about most of the work I was doing. The spaces I had designed had been built and were being lived in. I walked on carpets I'd selected for the lounges and offices and sat on the chairs I'd chosen. I ate off the place mats that I'd had designed for in-flight food service.

I made mistakes. The fabric selected for the San Juan airport lounge turned out to be too light and the chair seats had to be reupholstered. The carpet chosen for another lounge stained so badly after a week it had to be pulled up. But even the mistakes were okay, because they taught me more about how to do a job right than doing the job right. I enjoyed working and feeling like a capable person and I looked forward to Mondays.

Working was great, except for my guilt about the kids. It nagged at my conscience that they were not really getting enough parenting. I worried that they had lost not only their father, but their mother as well. I had changed. I was away a lot. I was tired in the evenings, and came home exhausted when I traveled. So much just slid by. We had less money, so we had less stuff. When I worried, I got edgy and made things worse. There was so much more I felt I should be giving them that I was really surprised when Miles turned to me as I drove him to school and said, "You know, we really have it pretty good." At first I thought he was being sarcastic, and when I realized he was serious, I knew that what he said was true.

Gradually I stopped feeling so shitty about all the things I couldn't get done by myself. I stopped thinking of my kids as being one rung up from orphans. I tried to get better at what I could do. I paced myself and set a careful course. And I could tell that I was in the groove, which is that point in sailing when you have just enough wind on either side of the sheet. It is that point when you are heading up toward your landmark, close to the wind and balanced and using everything you've got.

As I healed on the surface, I also healed within. I stopped dreaming about death. My subconscious began to support the direction of my recovery.

One morning I was awakened by the overwhelming aroma of coffee. It was so strong that I woke up immediately and got out of bed. It was four o'clock. I went over to the window and looked out to see who was up at that hour brewing coffee. I was exhausted and annoyed that someone had awakened me. There were no lights on anywhere on the block. The neighborhood was silent and asleep. The smell of coffee overpowered me. I was totally awake.

I lay down, still wide awake and still smelling the coffee. Shit, I thought, I'll never get to sleep now. And then, surprisingly, I fell into a short, dream-dominated drift of sleep.

Bob was sitting with me in the living room. He was in the last stages of leukemia and was thin and weak and pale. We were drinking coffee. He said, "You're doing everything just right. You must be a terrific person."

I looked around and saw Charlie, one of Bob's old friends, passing by at the end of the hallway. "Charlie, Charlie," I called. "Look, Bob's here."

Charlie looked at me and when I read the shock and sorrow on his face, the image of the pine coffin suspended over the hole flashed before me like a neon sign and I knew that I had buried Bob ten months before. I turned to look where Bob had been sitting and, of course, he wasn't there. I woke up. It was only a few minutes after four and there was no trace of the aroma of coffee.

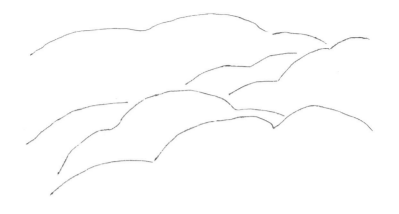

PART THREE

11

When I pulled the shmates off the mirrors seven days after Bob died, I could perceive no change in myself. I saw the same old girl. Nothing seemed to have happened. Bob had died and he had been buried, but nothing had changed. I felt strangely detached from the whole business, detached and unaffected. And for a long time after, whenever I thought about myself, I could not see myself as different. I didn't want it to have happened. I didn't want to perceive any impact, and perception is one of the few things we can control.

"Remember Ellie, that reporter with the big tits they moved down from Fort Lauderdale?" Bob asked years ago as we drove to a *Herald* party. "Well, she got this fantastic promotion. She's my editor now, and do you know what she did as soon as she got to be the boss?"

"No, I don't know. What did she do?"

"She grew a mustache."

I started to laugh, but he continued seriously as he weaved through traffic. "She grew a fucking mustache. I mean, it's not a great mustache. It's really more like adolescent peach fuzz now, but you can tell that if she started shaving, it would really fill in nicely. Yes, old Ellie finally got a little authority and it changed her entire hormonal balance. She grew a Goddamn mustache."

When I ran into Ellie at the party I couldn't keep my eyes off her upper lip. She did have a shadow of hair over her mouth, but she had always had that. It was no darker, no thicker than it had been when she was a reporter. Bob hadn't noticed it then, but once she became his boss he grew sensitive to every change in her behavior and appearance. The soft hair on her face dominated his perception and began to epitomize the change. He scribbled a mustache on the image in his mind and really believed it was there.

I did the opposite. I mentally erased all marks of change and sealed the image I had of myself like a fine wood floor. I really believed that my carefully preserved self-image wouldn't show any signs of what had happened, that it wouldn't show scuffs, that it wouldn't show single.

But in the year that followed it became apparent to others that I had changed, that I had evolved and remade myself to cope with my changed circumstances. You cannot be the person alone that you were in the pair, and if you think you can, just go visit an old friend, or your parents, or really examine your relationship with your kids. They see the difference clearly. And in case you are insensitive or totally blind to the fact that you have changed, in case you think you can truck along in your same old skin, they'll set you straight. They'll show you who you are with a jab, or with a slight, or with a stream of tears.

Change is always difficult. It takes a lot of energy. It is stressful and agonizingly slow. Change should be orchestrated and spread out and taken only in small, accountable, professionally monitored doses. It seemed that if I could just keep myself together, if I could just be unaffected by events, if I could just maintain my course, my personality, my style, I wouldn't have to suffer any more changes.

It seemed simple enough. But what I couldn't understand was why everyone else was acting so differently. My kids were getting out of control, communication between my parents and me was increasingly strained, and my friends had deserted me. What was wrong with them? Couldn't they see that I needed their cooperation, their support, their consistency? It was hard for me to understand why they had all defected at once, just at the very time I needed them.

Admittedly, the script was different, but that was no big deal. Only one character in the plot had been dropped. That certainly was no reason for everyone to lose interest. I was sure that I could keep the show on the road by doing some minor editing, but I was wrong about that. After a death, more than editing is required to hold the old audience's attention. And the audience is not necessarily amused by the revisions. The audience may not even be interested. The audience may just walk out the door. The changes in script did not disguise the fact that I was no longer the same. I wasn't your favorite couple at a dinner party. I wasn't your well-rested friend up for a good time. I wasn't your happily married daughter. I wasn't your mommy-chauffeur-tutor-nurse-servant-maid-cook. I wasn't your best friend's wife.

It took me a long time to get a clear picture of who I was without Bob. I did not feel that my identity as a woman had been changed by Bob's death. This illusion was encouraged by the lack of symbols and ceremony attached to the event of being widowed.

When Bob was writing his guidebook to Portugal, we traveled extensively through a part of the world that has a borderline personality. Portugal can just barely pass itself off as twentieth-century Europe. It is a religious and traditional country, proud, sad, and unique. In the village of Nazaré, on the Atlantic Ocean, the qualities of the country are distilled and have an immediate impact on the traveler. The fishermen of the village begin their day by going out to sea in long wooden boats. These boats are dragged back ashore at the end of their trips by teams of oxen. The water in Nazaré is rough and dangerous and you could tell that a lot of the fishermen didn't make it back, because every other woman in the city was a widow. You could tell that they were widows because they wore black.

I wore blue to the funeral. I didn't have a black dress and my mother said that blue was okay. It was okay. Probably nobody noticed or cared that another symbolic gesture had bitten the dust. But a symbol is a symbol of something, and if it works it does tend to point you in the direction of reality. I really was a widow and this really was different from being a wife and I really was changed by the events. I think if there had been some symbol to remind me of the change, I would have been more prepared for it. Perhaps I would have handled things better had it been made clear from the start that I was no longer a wife, that I was, in fact, a widow. Death had changed *me*, not the people who acknowledged that change.

I was bucking the tide when I tried to slip back into the same old scene. It became painfully clear—word by word, action by action, choice by choice—that the wife had been buried along with her husband. But she had been entombed without official mourning and without a ceremony to mark her own passing.

"If I were single," I told my sister, "I'd probably find a nice comfortable bar to hang out at and everyone would get to know me there and know that I would be there and it would become my own public sitting room."

Eileen stared at me for a while and finally said, "Hey, Bonnie, I hate to break it to you, but you *are* single."

12

The 727 approached Miami from the west. I looked down at the marbleized surface of the Everglades as we began our descent. The swamp was oozy green and absolutely flat. We usually come into Miami from that direction, heading into the prevailing easterly breezes to land, and when we do we fly over the cemetery where Bob is buried. The landing gear made its familiar thud as the stewardess passed through the cabin one last time. I could see little white marks lined up rhythmically on the landscape below. They made Lakeview Memorial Park look like a miniature stringently zoned neighborhood at the edge of the city. The no-smoking sign appeared as we flew over a new construction site. Another batch of town houses was on the way up. Another rash of temporary residences was closing in on the cemetery and on the swamp.

Two days of design work in New York had drained me. I headed home, and when I opened the door I was greeted first by the smell coming from the cat box. Next came a "Wadja get me" from Asher. The television was blaring and some popcorn crunched under my feet as I walked by Seth and Asher without a word and dragged my bag up to the bedroom—which was a mess. One of the kids had taken a nap in my bed after school and left his dirty socks on top of the rumpled sheets. I picked up the socks and took them to the hamper, passing Miles studying in his room. On the chair next to him was the pile of laundry he had taken in off the line. In the morning a huddle would form around this pile as each kid tried to find some clean clothes for school.

After taking a quick shower in what little bit of hot water was left, I went down to the kitchen and found that Seth had washed the dishes but left the floor flooded and that Asher had changed the litter box but left a trail of sand leading to the back door. What pissed me off, though, what really got me to blow my cool and forget how hard everyone was trying, was when I got to the refrigerator and discovered that my kids had polished off the Häagen-Dazs.

The details always got to me. If "God is in the details," then so is his opposite number. It was always a detail that made me nuts. All the bases were covered but so thinly that any normal mishap read FOUL on the scoreboard in bright lights. The kids were used to it. Mommy came home from a trip and she was tired and then she freaked out about some dumb thing and then she was okay. They probably placed bets on what would do the trick. Maybe the refrigerator door would be left open, or the tub would overflow and drip water into the kitchen, or the washing machine wouldn't drain.

It was easy to get upset about the details because that's all they were. I could work off my steam on the little things and not have to see the real problems that were screaming for attention. I was big on denial. I didn't want to admit that this terrible thing had happened and that I had been affected by it. I didn't want anything to disturb my illusion of calm. "Oh, God, no ice cream," I could say, as if that were the only problem I had to contend with.

But the children became my barometers. I began to read "warning" into the rapid drop in their spirits, and as I responded to them I could feel how drastically the climate of our relationship had changed.

In my living room there is a copper pot filled with photographs. For years I have been tossing snapshots into the pot, and every once in a while I sit down and go through these pictures. They have become catalysts for remembering and ordering the past. One photograph leads to the next and a story unfolds. When I look at them, I can plot our progress like a hurricane tracker who sees in retrospect where the storm has been, but can only guess where it is heading.

You can almost smell a baby when you look at the photograph. The infant is asleep in his sterile hospital bassinet. His eyes are closed and the thin strands of hair on his head have been gently oiled and brushed forward. He is curled up, tightfisted, under a blue blanket. There is a card on the side of the glass bassinet that says LISS BOY 7 lbs., 11 oz.

I am holding Miles in my arms. He is a month old. His chin is resting on my upper arm as he peers over with big eyes into the lens of the camera. He looks divine. I am gazing at him with absolute adoration. We could be posing for a portrait of Jesus and Mary except for my haircut. My hair is definitely too short. It is the exact cut that members of the Resistance gave to French women who were caught sleeping with Nazis.

Miles came first. He was the first and so he was the reason —the reason to become parents, the reason to normalize our lives. He was the one who threw the track as we barreled along our unconventional 1960s way. We had been heading due left, and he threw the switch and changed our routing to the right.

I was surprised to find that I could fill the role of mother so effectively and on such short notice. One day he wasn't there and the next day he was. One day I was welding sculptures in my garage studio in Boston and the next day I was embroidering bibs. My IQ must have dropped about forty points after his birth. I organized every minute of my day around him. I made him mobiles and toys and wrote little children's books for him and about him. I fed him whenever he was hungry. I gave him carefully timed sunbaths every day and pushed his carriage all over Boston looking for fresh fruit and vegetables to steam or blend into pulp. Gerber's wasn't good enough for my little boy. I called my pediatrician daily to make sure that Miles really wouldn't die of diaper rash, prickly heat, or failure to burp. And when nothing was unusual, I called the pediatrician to tell him that all was well.

I am squinting into the camera and trying to hold Miles steady as he squirms in my arms. He is three months old and is already annoyed with being held and frustrated by his limitations. His back is stiff and he is holding himself as far away from me as possible.

Bob is walking with his son up on his shoulders. Miles is one year old. He has let go of the grip he had on his father's hair to pose nicely for the picture. Bob is trying to give me his sensitive James Dean look, even though his head is bent forward under the weight of the child. Miles is sitting up straight and proud, smiling happily at me. He is just where he wants to be—with his papa.

Miles is standing in a pair of underpants with two fingers in his mouth and a piece of a blue baby blanket under his arm. He is two and a half years old. I have just retrieved the blanket from the garbage can outside our cottage. He threw it there by himself. He wanted to get rid of the blanket, to cut himself off from this dependence. In a show of strength he had taken the blanket, marched stoically out the door to the dumpster, and thrown it in. He went to bed cold turkey, and only when his howls began to affect his ability to breathe did I go out with a flashlight to find the piece of blanket. The picture catches the boy clinging ambivalently to his baby-hood, grateful that I had retrieved it, angry that he had weakened. Tears of defeat are standing in his eyes.

Miles was his father's boy from the start. I was his mother but Bob was his closest relative. They had their own communication. Bob was on the path he couldn't wait to run down and follow. And he was ready to follow it wherever it went, no questions asked. He was ready to go at three months, one year, two and a half. You could see it in the photographs. If only he were mobile, if only he were verbal, if only he didn't need those arms, that blanket, that breast. He was ready to go and he pulled away from me as if I were the very dependence he resented, as if I were the source of his helplessness. This is terrific and correct and what we all hope for in a child. This is shitty. Can't he see how fragile he still is, I still am?

Seth is propped up in an infant seat on the kitchen table. I have just brought him home from the hospital. Miles is seventeen months old. He has climbed up on a chair and leans onto the table to see what the excitement is all about. Their eyes meet. Miles' mouth falls open at the sight of the baby. His eyes are saucers, filled with confusion. Seth is cool. He has stopped crying for the first time all day and looks straight at Miles with level gray eyes. His tiny features are perfectly poised as he meets his brother.

The young man is holding his two sons. The older one is caught out of focus as he struggles to get down. Fifteen seconds in one spot is enough for him. If the old lady can't take a picture by then, the hell with it. Seth is immobile, cradled in his father's arm. He is two months old. His eyes are half closed and he looks very sleepy. He should look sleepy. He has been up all night crying. He is in perfect focus. There is nowhere he wants to go, and he melts into his father's arm and his brother rushes down to play.

Seth is posed next to Miles. He is ten months old and we are getting ready to move to Israel. Bob wanted to take one last picture. Miles has a full head of hair, stylishly cut, and big brown eyes. Seth is totally bald, has two chins and no neck. He cries in misery as he is lined up next to his brother. He will keep on crying until I pick him up and hold him tight and give back his pacifier.

Seth came second. He was very different from his brother. He loved to be held and taken care of. He was a real dependent, happily tied to his mommy for as long as she would have him. Seth was my papoose, and he howled between hugs, protesting the isolation of infancy.

We moved out of the country before he was a year old. I was pregnant for the third time but Bob decided we were too young to settle down and should have a few more adventures. The options for adventure are limited when you have a pregnant wife and two babies. Moving to a kibbutz—a collective farm—in Israel was actually a logical choice. I didn't really want to go. I wrote to the Israeli government requesting a kibbutz where the children spent the day in children's houses but slept at home, where there were lots of Americans to socialize with, and—most important of all —where there was a view of the Mediterranean.

I never expected them to take me seriously. I thought they would send me a brochure from the Tel Aviv Hilton. But a few weeks later we were given the name of an appropriate farm and within two months we were on a ship heading to a place called Gesher Haziv, which was full of Americans, had a view of the Mediterranean, and had accommodations for children to live at home. It was also only a few miles away from the Lebanese border.

Seth, who was renamed "Shai," is standing against the brightly painted gate at his children's house on the kibbutz. He is a year old and thin blond hair is beginning to cover his head. He has a pacifier in each hand and one in his mouth. His nose is running. Shai is watching me intently, hoping this day will be different, hoping I won't turn and leave, hoping I will find him irresistible and come back and lift him over the gate and take him to our cottage or to the beach or for a bus ride into Nahariya. He sucks frantically on the pacifier that is in his mouth and squeezes the other two between his fingers as I snap the picture.

Shai is standing in front of a horde of children with a wreath of flowers in his hair. Everyone in the picture is dressed up and wearing wreaths. It is Hag Habikorrim, which is the Israeli celebration of the picking of the first fruits. On this holiday the firstborn in each family is honored and decked in flowers. Shai is not really my firstborn, but I made him a wreath anyway. He smiles broadly while the genuine first fruits run around, a bewreathed blur in the background.

Shai is sitting on Bob's lap in front of our cottage. He is smiling a very contagious smile. It has even spread to the tired face of his father, who spent the day pruning avocado trees. It spreads to whoever looks at the photograph. He is two years old, top dog in the children's house, and popular with everyone on the kibbutz because he is so open and loving and happy. His hair is almost white and it frames his glowing face like rays around the sun.

Shai means "gift" in Hebrew, and this turned out to be a very fitting name. The kibbutzniks had their doubts at first, but once his nose stopped running, his hair grew in, and he finally stopped crying, they had to admit Shai was a real gift. And for Shai, life in a village environment was a gift too. It was the gift of abundant adult attention. He felt secure and important within the community. It was also a gift to be able to spend his days with babies like himself and out from under the shadow of his brother.

"Micha" is wearing a pair of overalls and a flannel shirt. He is four years old. Miles has been called Micha since our move to Israel. He speaks fluent Hebrew and broken English. He is on his way for a hike with his father. They will go out to the grove and pick some fine ripe fruit to bring back for us. Micha cocks his head to one side and looks proudly into the camera. His hands are on his hips and his hair is long and wild.

Asher is propped up in an infant seat. His arms are lifted up and the sunlight bounces off his tiny fists. He is a month old and is my most peaceful baby. He is everyone's most peaceful baby, in fact, and on the kibbutz where he was born he is known as "Asher m'ooshar"—happy Asher. When I snapped the picture I was unaware that the sunlight filtering in through the window would give the image on the photograph a haunting transparency.

I could barely remember being pregnant the third time. I was so busy with the other two kids and with preparing for the move to Israel that I could easily have forgotten I had even been pregnant. Except that four years later the doctors asked me over and over to think back and try to recall if anything unusual had happened during my pregnancy with Asher. Was I absolutely sure, they would ask, that I hadn't *taken anything?* This question came right after the assurance that I had nothing to feel guilty about. Hell, I hadn't even thought about feeling guilty until they put it to me for the fifteenth time. "Are you absolutely certain, Mrs. Liss, that you didn't do anything unusual during this pregnancy?"

What was unusual? Was it unusual to chicken out of buying your first house? Was it unusual to move to a collective farm halfway around the world? Was it unusual to work painting Disneyesque murals in bomb shelters? And since when was it a crime to "do anything unusual"?

The two-year-old child is studying the movement of a sprinkler head. He taps it rhythmically into motion. He has been absorbed with this sprinkler since he finished breakfast three hours earlier. Asher looks up at me with his calm and unblinking stare as I snap the picture. An aura of silence surrounds the child.

The boys are lined up in front of an orange tree and they almost look like triplets. They have identical early-Beatles haircuts and they are wearing identical red gingham shirts. Micha and Shai are both smiling so broadly that their eyes are cheeked shut. Asher is looking at me with his open stare. His eyes are vacant, waiting to be filled with whatever you imagine. He could be a saint. He could be a Martian. I could peddle photographs of this child on a street in Greenwich Village.

Something was wrong. I had read Spock and Piaget and I knew that something was really wrong. We moved back to the United States to get some help for him. Israel was recovering from a war. Kneecaps and faces had to be rebuilt.

Doctors didn't have the time or energy for finding the key to a little boy with a short circuit.

Asher was really different. He started to talk at a respectable age but switched gears when he was around two. He gave up speech for animal and mechanical sounds, and after a few months he gave those up for silence. By the time he was four he was completely nonverbal and had practically stopped growing. He was like little Oscar in *The Tin Drum*, only instead of banging on a drum, Asher flushed toilets. Wherever we went, be it to a friend's house or a supermarket or a department store, Asher would head straight for the toilet and begin flushing. He could find the most carefully camouflaged crapper. Had there been a toilet at the end of the labyrinth, Asher could have beaten Theseus through the maze.

What is amazing about children who do not develop like everyone else isn't so much the differences they exhibit as the way they dramatize our incredible sameness. We grow up alike and unyielding, ready to tromp on any disparity that crosses our path.

We were told to put him in an institution. We were told he wouldn't develop and would always be a burden. We were told to think about the rest of the family. We were told to dump him for being different. I couldn't believe it. It seemed audacious to me that such a slim range of behavior was considered tolerable, and that if a child took steps out of this range he would be subject to a systematic pecking that makes birds look like saints. There is a fine line between sanity and insanity, and Asher perched himself right on that line like a tightrope artist who had lost the courage to finish the walk.

Asher was finally diagnosed as having some autistic tendencies, and the diagnosis helped to get him into a serious and constructive program at Mailman Institute in Miami. He was lucky. In 1974 autism was the syndrome of the year.

Programs and sensitive therapists were available. Had it been ten years earlier or had he been diagnosed as retarded or schizophrenic, he would probably still be flushing toilets.

Miles and Seth are sitting in the living room of our house in Miami Beach. We have just moved in. There are no curtains or shades on the windows yet, so the sun pours in uncontrolled and bleaches out the background. The image of the boys stands out clearly against the apparent emptiness. Seth looks away from the camera and his face is resolute. His bare shoulders, outlined by whiteness, look crisp and fragile. Miles has an arm around his brother and smiles confidently from the sun-filled room.

Asher is sitting under a large tropical bush in front of our house. He is almost five years old and he is almost smiling. You can see that he is pleased with himself. This is a new feeling, so he holds back and only almost smiles. He began speaking earlier in the day. We were at a stoplight and when it changed he said, "green light." I thought that I was hearing things, but when I slowed down for a yield sign, he said, "triangle." This picture will always say to me, "Asher, on the day he began talking."

For a few years there were no pictures. Bob got sick, and the passage of time was something none of us had the heart to record. The pictures taken after his death are hard to look at.

Miles is scowling into the camera. He is twelve years old. My father has come to Miami to try to cheer us up. He has taken us to Castle Park, which is a favorite with the kids, but everyone is miserable. Bob has been dead for six months. Miles is doing me a favor by looking into the camera. He has just finished cheating at miniature golf, kicking Seth, and

*telling Asher to shut up. In a few minutes he will bump into
an old lady by accident and shove her out of his way. I will
grab him by the hair and smack him in the face. But at that
moment, as the camera snaps, he is merely giving me his "I
smell shit" look. Tables with aluminum umbrellas dot the
concrete patio on which he is standing, and a phony castle
looms in the background.*

All Miles needed was a safety pin in his earlobe to complete the picture. He was a punk. I could have rented him
out to the campaign for birth control. He shoved and
scowled. His anger turned physical as he bulldozed his way
through the maze he found himself in. He was left without a
route, without a guide, and without a psychological barrier
against his own mortality.

His hostile behavior was a cry for help. He needed something, and my reaction surprised me. I had always been so
anxious to mother the boy, but then I couldn't seem to drum
up that emotion. I had changed, and it wasn't until Miles
needed the old me that I realized how profound the change
had been. If babying would have helped, if he needed to be
lavished with attention and affection to regain his bearings,
then he was in trouble. I had lost my ability to play the old
mother role. For one thing, it is hard to give when you are
flat broke. I was not in an emotional position to offer much
to anybody. And besides, the necessary assumption of responsibility had robbed me of the "mind" that mothers. I
was tough and efficient and decisive all day, and when I
came home I was the parent, which is much different from
being the "better half."

As a child I always knew which problems to take to my
mother and which to take to my father. My parents were
very different and had been able to let their differences
polarize into two attitudes, each of which made sense or

worked only because of the presence of the other. But once you are the whole show you cannot be the supporting act. George Burns used to end his show with a drag on his cigar and a "Say goodnight, Gracie." The audience laughed every week at the homey combination of condescension and affection. Then she would stop babbling long enough to say "Goodnight, Gracie." It was positively endearing, that dumb-broad "goodnight." She never could have said it like that if he hadn't set her up. She would have had to devise another routine to get the laugh alone if, alone, she still cared about getting that laugh.

It was impossible for me to mother Miles out of his anger in the same way that I had mothered him through other crises. I had assumed a new role and I wasn't sure how to fit all the responsibilities together so they made sense to him. He couldn't all of a sudden look up to and emulate the very person he had always worked to be free of, the very person whose endearing dumb-broad remarks made him roll his eyes just like his father did.

Seth is standing with his friend Jimmy Koenig. Jimmy is posing nicely, smiling into the lens of my camera. Seth indulges me by standing semi-still. He is a lanky eleven-year-old with poor posture. The boys were on their way to Jimmy's house, and Seth is anxious to go. He has no time for theatrics. The camera snaps, catching Jimmy smiling and Seth out of focus, moving to get away.

Seth was pulling away. He felt betrayed. First, he was born a middle child; second, his father had died; and third, his mother didn't seem to have any time for him. He drifted off with his friends. Every Friday afternoon he'd call from John's or Jimmy's with the same request.

"Can I sleep over?"

"You slept over last weekend. Come on home."

"Oh please," he'd say, "he's already asked his mother. Please."

"Okay, but be home first thing in the morning."

And if he got home in time for supper, I was doing well. I let this go on because it made him happy and because I had one fewer kid to worry about. If it had stopped with a rejection of the family, I wouldn't have been worried. I had done the same thing at his age. I had stepped out on my family whenever I could and developed relationships with my friends that seemed infinitely more meaningful at the time. But Seth turned on himself as well and began to sabotage his ability to learn and succeed.

Bonnie, B.D. (Before Death), was a watchful mother, involved in the kids' day-to-day development. She checked homework, quizzed spelling, and went to PTA meetings, ensuring that extra bit of teachery concern.

Bonnie, A.D. (After Death), was a single parent, a mother by gender. She came home from work tired, and when she traveled she didn't come home from work at all. She didn't check homework—heck, she didn't *ask* about homework, and when it came to spelling, you had to quiz yourself. PTA meetings weren't even considered.

Some kids can function very well without a lot of attention and feedback, and some kids cannot. Seth had a fragile ego, and the direction of my change seemed like one more personal blow. He gave up. By the time he was twelve, he had worked himself into the lowest track of classes in Dade County. He could barely construct a sentence. He had trouble with history, was a disaster in math, and almost flunked science.

What could I do? I had to work, I had to travel. I always seemed to come home tired and with little patience for the kids. I could curse my dilemma and the terrible quality of education in Dade County, but that wouldn't change the situation.

Seth was a bright kid. The problem was that he no longer believed it. You could see the uncertainty in his eyes, in his posture. You could feel the uneasiness as he walked by. A glass of milk would topple over in anticipation when he entered a room. His problems intensified as I grew more detached. He could never seem to get his homework right. He would do the wrong page with the wrong color ink and turn it in on the wrong day. I didn't help him with his homework because I would get impatient or because I was out of town or because I was just out.

Note: to be read aloud by a very serious child

IT'S ELEVEN AT NIGHT.

DO YOU KNOW WHERE YOUR MOTHER IS?

I was never home. I couldn't stand to be there. I felt betrayed by the very structure that housed our family. Every crack, every patch of peeling paint screamed out that I was alone now and that I couldn't handle it. I was Seth's role model for staying away.

It wasn't just the house. Doing things with the boys reminded me how alone I really was with them, so I stopped being available. If I wrote myself out of the script, I didn't have to notice how much it had changed. It was only as their problems developed that I began to see how my attempt at denial was affecting us all.

My excuse had been that there was no time for the kids, but really the time was there. It just had to be salvaged. I forced myself to do things with them. At first I was on edge when we stayed at home together. I lost my appetite when we went out to dinner, and there seemed to be a rash of boring movies. Turning things around wasn't easy. The cop-out had become comfortable.

My adjustment at work had been easy compared with my

adjustment at home. The more I put into my work, the more I learned and the better I became at it. But the more I did with my kids, the worse we seemed to get at being a family. They fought with each other constantly. No matter what we did there was always the inevitable fight that would ruin the day. They were opposing teams and I was the miserable referee, accused of bias by each side. And then I discovered something. I didn't have to do things with all three kids at once. I could do things with them one at a time. They didn't seem to mind this arrangement at all and were surprisingly patient for their turn. When it came, there was no one to compete with or fight with or show off for.

Asher didn't bother to look up for his school photograph. His hair is a tangle of curls and his eyes look exhausted. I'm not sure which class he is posing with. I had pushed to have him taken out of his learning disabilities class for part of the day and mainstreamed into a regular fourth grade. The only thing he managed to learn in the year after his father's death was to hate school.

What was my problem? The kid had been developing slowly but steadily. Why was I pushing things, especially then, so soon after Bob's death? I had always been patient. I had always been confident that he was progressing at a pace that made sense. So why was I being so unreasonable?

I was scared. I was responsible suddenly, and I was afraid that he would never develop enough to take care of himself and that I would always have to be there for him even when I got old. Nothing had changed. That had always been a possibility, but it never frightened me while Bob was alive. He was the responsible party. I could afford to be patient and sensitive and let him be the bad guy and do the nasty worrying.

I was so obsessed with Asher's development that I pushed

him into a situation he wasn't ready for, hoping he would prove me wrong. He didn't. When he couldn't make it in the fourth grade, I became even more frantic and threatened to sue the school system if they tried to put him back. I was afraid he might never be ready for the fourth grade or the fifth grade or adulthood. I had been patient and sensible as a wife but not as a parent. Alone, with so much responsibility, I lost my instinct for the child. I tried to hasten his development and made everything much worse. At the end of the year, I began to see what was happening and allowed him to be returned to his special class, where he was able to regain his bearings and begin to learn again at his own careful pace.

I am standing next to Miles. He has just finished his Bar Mitzvah, which marks his first adult participation in Judaism. He is thirteen years old. I am wearing a very expensive white-and-lilac outfit. I traded in a car to buy the dress. On my head is a little cranberry straw hat.

Miles is wearing a dark-blue suit that he will outgrow within the hour. We have our arms around each other and are smiling together. I look like one of the Pointer Sisters in my getup.

Miles had picked out the hat as I was buying the dress. "Get the hat, Mom," he said. "It'll really make it. The dress is nice but it needs this hat."

"Forty dollars for a hat! I don't ever wear hats. I'll only wear it once. I mean, when am I ever going to wear a hat?"

"So what? Get the hat. It'll make the outfit. You'll look great. Get the hat. I insist."

I got the hat. The service is over. He didn't make any mistakes. He had written his own speech and talked about losing faith after his father's death and then regaining it in time for his Bar Mitzvah. He didn't mention how terribly frustrating it had been as the emotional dust slowly settled and he finally began to feel comfortable with himself and with the only parent he had.

Seth and I are having dinner together at the Miamarina. He is twelve years old. We are sitting outside on the patio close to the docks. It is September and Seth is talking opti- mistically about the school year. After a year on the brink of child abuse, I found a tutor to work on his study habits and help him with his homework. He is back in the more demand- ing classes and proud of himself for being there. His initial success snowballed into a real interest in learning.

"Oh, my history class is so cool," he said. "Did you know that the Eskimos came from Asia? See, there was the land bridge, and the animals went over first looking for food and then the Asians followed them."

A photographer working the restaurant came over and asked if we would like a picture together, and Seth said, "Sure." He is caught sitting straight up in his chair, grin- ning over a plate of fish, as I lift a drink to the Eskimos.

The three pictures were taken in one day. Asher is ten years old. In the first picture he is fishing off the end of a dock, looking intently at the water, oblivious of the camera. In the second photograph Asher is holding up a fish that he caught. It is about eight inches long, but the smile on his face makes it look a lot longer. Asher would know how to clean the fish when he got home. A friend of mine, Glenn, taught Asher how to do it, and he is almost as proud of his ability to clean them as he is to catch them.

"Mom," he asked as I focused the camera for the third shot, "is Glenn older than you or younger than you?"

"He's younger than me. Why?"

"Well, good, 'cause then he can take care of you when you get old and I won't have to."

I looked at him in surprise and then took the third picture, which is of a relieved little fisherman cleaning dinner for his family.

It was up and down. We did well and we did terribly, but the family survives. The family can survive hopping on one foot. It has a history and it has dependencies and loves and loyalties that give it a strength no other unit possesses. An earlier admission of the impact of Bob's death might have made the necessary adjustments a lot easier, but even without that recognition the family survives. It may be strained and hurt, but it weathers the blows like the coconut palms along the shore that yield knowingly to the pressure of a storm.

13

The relationship between my parents and me was affected more by my husband's death than it had been by our marriage. Marriage hadn't changed much. They never lost their daughter. But with Bob's death, something of the girl was lost too, and when that happened the family portrait was not the same. I had been raised for a way of living that wasn't an option anymore. I was making adjustments that they hadn't counted on and couldn't always react to with the grace they always had for the expected. I was no longer my mother's married daughter or my father's dependent once removed.

The summer after Bob died, my mother flew down to help me pack the kids for camp. We ran out to the department store for some last-minute items. It felt comfortable to be shopping together and we were having a good old mother-daughter time.

"You know," she suddenly said, "I made a mistake. I should have been much more religious all my life."

My mother had always been tolerant of religion but never

really into it, so her announcement surprised me. It was a change of pace, and I went for it, hoping to connect with a genuine spiritual perception.

"Oh, yeah? Why? What do you mean?"

"Well, if I had been more religious, then you probably would have been more religious, and it's easier to meet a decent man at your age if you're involved in religion."

I stopped next to a mannequin in a flowered duster. Everything looked yellow and flat under the fluorescent lighting that glared from the ceiling of the store. I coaxed my legs back into motion and trudged, disheartened, toward the boys' department.

My mother has always been satisfied with being a full-time housewife. She had six children, my father made a good living, and that went a long way in the 1950s. There was no reason for her even to think about working in any terms except "Thank God, I don't have to."

Her mother had worked. When she was little, my mother didn't know what she did all day, but she thought it had something to do with streetcars. Every morning she watched her mother, Clara, get on the streetcar and disappear. In the evening the streetcar would bring her mommy home. For all she knew, Clara rode around the streets of Chicago and made sure that nobody put their feet on the furniture or chewed with their mouths open or fought with their brothers.

Clara didn't work because she wanted to establish her identity through meaningful employment. She worked because her husband died and left her with three young children and seventeen cents. She had no particular skills and could not speak English. She didn't work on the streetcar. The streetcar took her to and from Hart, Schaffner & Marx, where she spent sixteen years sewing labels on suits.

My mother didn't ever want to have to work for a living, and she didn't want to see her daughters work for a living either. She wanted us married and supported, and if we couldn't manage to achieve that by our twenty-first birthday, there was always graduate school. If nothing panned out in graduate school, well, she supposed we'd screwed up somehow and would have to go to work.

In 1969 my mother did something that surprised everyone. She decided to go to college and learn a profession. She spent three years getting an associate degree that qualified her as a medical technician. She got straight As and we were all very proud of her. She never took a job, though.

"Your father wants me here when he gets home or takes time off," she said, "and, besides, I really only did it because I had this fantasy of helping out your brothers in their medical practice. But they both became psychiatrists and don't need a technician."

She had learned a profession to help out her sons. She would have worked only to extend herself as a mother, not to feel productive in any newly liberated way or even to make money as her mother had done. And since my brothers didn't need her anymore, she stayed at home and kept it perfect for my father.

So how could I expect my mother to see my situation as anything but pathetic? In the first place, my husband had died, and in the second, I had to work. To make matters worse, I seemed to be adjusting. And the more I adjusted, the more it bothered her, because I was losing my desperate instinct to find a man to take care of me. I was getting picky. My sister was picky too.

Pop Quiz: Choose the phrase that most accurately describes my sister Eileen.

A. She is not even thirty years old and she is already executive producer for the CBS news in St. Louis.

B. She is already thirty years old and she is not even married.

If B is chosen, a strong sympathy is displayed for my

mother's point of view. Sometimes even my sister chooses B. A mother's expectations and disappointments can be joked about and argued over, but they cannot be disregarded as irrelevant because they become our own measuring stick. I was working because I was single with three kids to support. It was a good job, *but* it would be better if I were married and didn't have to work. The pride that my mother felt in what I did was always blunted by a "but," and I have to constantly battle this "but" in the image I have of myself.

Before the "but," I had been my mother's married daughter. I was the one who didn't have to be sent to graduate school. I was the one who had been living by her very code, who had been proving that "God was right about that." And then, at thirty-five, I became a liability. I became another daughter to be married off, an aging daughter with three kids and picky yet.

A word of criticism from my mother sends me into an amplified depression. I know that I am able to handle things well and am becoming a successful parent and woman. Still, with a single sigh she can spark off in me a welling of insecurity and incompleteness. I feel so vulnerable to her concerns and fears because they are my own. I learned so much from her. We have the same dragons.

Before the "but," approval had been so simple. I could just sit home and be Mrs. Robert Liss. And even if the house was a mess, the kids were flunking study hall, and my husband was carrying on with the copygirl, I had my mother's approval. She always felt that I was doing just fine. I was living the life she had chosen as right for herself and for everyone she cared about, and I picked up on her positive attitude and was encouraged.

But it happened. My husband died and I went to work, and her attitude toward me changed because in her mind a woman who works for a living is a woman who would rather be doing something else. She sees my ability to carry a job as something I have to do until I get married again. She cannot be as supportive as she had been. She cannot approve.

Flash—Clara climbs onto a streetcar. Her long drab coat just cuts the morning chill. A sun is rising somewhere beyond the buildings. The trolley wheels grind out a metallic screech that echoes as she disappears into the windy city of Chicago.

Hey, I don't do that. I climb onto a 727 and disappear into the blue sky over Miami. It's a neat job. I wear Perry Ellis suits. But sometimes after a long trip with lots of unresolved problems, I get off the plane late at night, exhausted, discouraged, and I am greeted only by the dragon.

You need a husband to take care of you. This is fucking ridiculous. You blew it, kiddo.

By morning I am okay. I get up, take a shower, make coffee, wake the kids, give them breakfast, and do a load of laundry before we all rush off. I feel great. I like it close to the line, and I'm proud of myself and of all the things I can do. The dragon is back in its cage.

—How many Jewish daughters does it take to change a light bulb?

—Two. One to hold the Tab and one to call her father.

I used to call my father a lot. If we didn't have enough money to pay our property tax, I called my father and he sent a check. If my refrigerator went on the blink, I called my father and he sent a new one. If the kids needed clothes, I sent them to St. Louis in rags and without luggage. They always returned in suits and with checked baggage.

Bob fumed whenever I asked my father for something, but it never bothered me one bit. I wasn't the one who worked forty hours a week to support a family, so I never had to feel like a shmuck when we were in the red. "Big deal. So he sends us money. It gives him pleasure."

I wasn't bothered by asking my father for stuff, because I was already on the take. I had no personal income. My husband paid for everything. He paid for my food, my shelter, my blue jeans, my T-shirts, my oil paints, my clay, my books, my underwear, my tampons. He always magically laid out the cash and paid my way, so what did it really matter to me if Daddy picked up a tab or two for old time's sake?

We were finishing brunch in Miami Beach one winter afternoon. My parents had flown down for a visit. The waiter carefully placed the bill in the neutral zone between Bob and my father. Bob lunged for it.

"You're always taking us out," he said. "Let me get this one."

Both men had drawn their plastic. The waiter shuffled, waiting for one of them to make a move. I held my breath. My father deferred. He put his credit card back into his wallet. Bob smiled triumphantly at me and slid his card onto the waiter's tray. I smiled back but thought he was an asshole. If he had let my father grab the check, he would have had enough money to take me out to dinner one night later in the week.

I put an unreasonable value on a few bucks because the experience of earning and spending was totally beyond my scope. Money has a mystique to someone who doesn't work. People with money seem to possess a mysterious knowledge and ability. My kids get very quiet when I buy things or pay a bill. One wrong move, one sneeze, cough, or shuffle could break the spell that envelops the strange exchange of paper for stuff. I had this same awe all my life. Even after my marriage, I was still a little girl, reverent at that moment of payment so that the inscrutable rite of wampum would not be desecrated.

The mystique that had hung over making money, obscuring the process of exchange, was lifted by my first paycheck.

I had done a job, gotten what was promised, and exchanged that for what I needed. It was so simple. I didn't have to scramble or connive or hide in a bush and wait for a chicken to come along. I didn't have to pick berries or collect water. I didn't have to ask my father.

I was even able finally to give him something. My job with the airline allowed me some tremendous travel benefits that I could pass on to my parents. Want to fly to San Francisco, London, Hong Kong? Just give me a call, Dad, and I'll take care of it. Whatever you need, no strings attached. Don't be shy. It's my pleasure.

—How many parents of airline employees does it take to travel?

—Two. One to pack the carryon and one to call their daughter.

I stopped hitting my father for money, and by November I had enough to pay my property tax. It was the first time since we moved into the house that the actual owner had come up with the dough. I didn't have more money, but I was working for it. I put in my week, got my paycheck, and in order for it all to make sense, in order for me to have a tangible measure of success, it became very important that I pay my own way. I understood why Bob had fumed whenever I hit my old man for some money. It was saying, "Hey, I can't make it."

And more. Because as long as my father helped me out, I remained very much his little girl. Our relationship hadn't changed much in thirty-five years. He gave and I took. He never asked me for anything, but he did have a standard for my behavior. When I met his standard, I felt like I had been bribed. When I didn't meet it, I felt like a thief. As long as I was on the take, I was also on the hook, trapped by my feeling of obligation. My behavior didn't change when I began to support myself. What changed was my attitude. I

CRUISING AT 30,000 FEET

was finally nobody's dependent. The obligation I had always felt for the man with the bucks, I now felt for myself. I could react to my father honestly, and I began to see that he was really not the domineering force of my childhood. He was a concerned parent.

There was something else I began to notice about my father. He loved to work. I don't think he will ever retire. My grandfather never really retired either. He still goes to the store, chauffeured by his son, who had to de-car him after he drove in reverse up his driveway, across the street, and through a neighbor's picture window. Grandpa's reactions may have slowed as he aged, but his interest in the business is as active as ever. My father grew up with this positive perception of work. He has it for himself, for his sons, and for his daughters. He is supportive and proud of us all. Something does bother him about his daughters' working, though.

"My girls work much harder than my boys," I've heard him say, "but they don't make half as much. They may be smarter and more talented and more committed, but they'll always be paid less because they're women. It's not fair." He is hot on the subject. He sends me cartoons and clippings that deal with job discrimination and women. He supports the ERA. He is a quiet feminist.

As I changed, my parents made adjustments that were within their range of reactions. I was lucky because the sympathies were there, and the role model was there too. It was a matter of having the flexibility to find them. I know that I cannot expect my mother to change her perception of working women just because I have to work. And it is not essential for me to fight her dragon, just my own. My domineering father has turned out to be a supportive person and one with qualities I need to study.

The parents still function as parents. I have traded dependence for responsibility, habit for communication, and the balance between us is clearly better. The old patterns were broken, and as we put the pieces back together we are finally forming the base for a mature relationship.

14

Friends are different. Friends don't have to stick around. They don't have to celebrate holidays with you or toast you at weddings or remember your birthday or be nice to your kids. Friends don't have to see a lawyer when they want out. They can just disappear, and sometimes they do. Friends stick around because they want to, and the choice has two sides.

SIDE ONE

I ran into Franny in the second aisle of the supermarket. When she rounded the hot dog bin, I just froze. I wished that I had done my shopping a few hours earlier or had skipped the second aisle altogether, but there we were, cart to cart, surrounded by the cans, the boxes, the jars, and the silence.

She had been my best friend. We used to know absolutely everything about one another. I knew the details of her divorce and her love affairs. She knew when my marriage was up and when it was down. We once traded histories like old comic books, but it had been months since we last spoke. I had to say something. I couldn't just walk by.

"Franny, hi. You look great. Gee, I haven't seen you in a while. What's happening?"

"Bonnie, wow! I'm good. How are you doing? How are the kids?"

We were being polite. It was sickening. Her cart was filled with Coca-Cola, tonic, pretzels, and nuts. She was probably having a Goddamn party. She was probably having parties all the time, for all I knew.

"Well," she said, "I gotta hurry and get home. It's good to see you. Bye."

The checkout lines were long. It was winter and the population of Miami Beach had doubled for the season. Franny was in another line. I smiled at her and looked away. I looked at the bag boy. His face was covered with zits. I looked at the fat cashier. She poked at the keys of her register with sawed-off, nail-bitten fingers. I looked at the cover of the National Enquirer, *at anything that would keep me from looking back at Franny. I knew that if I looked at her again I would not smile. I would not be polite. I would walk over and slug her.*

I had read accounts of widows and how they lost their friends. I read that their buddies had dropped them one by one after their husband's death. I read all about it on airplanes when I got desperate enough to accept a women's magazine, but I never thought it would be my story too. I was so sure that my friends were different. They were so terrific, so unconventional. They were cool and they cared about me. But six months later they no longer existed.

I saw red when I ran into Franny. I was hurt and angry, not just at her but at the whole broken circle of friends. The people I used to see when Bob was alive had, for one reason or another, moved on, stopped calling. Maybe they thought

*that death was contagious. Maybe they had only liked Bob.
Maybe they were all a bunch of jerks.*

*I drove home and unloaded my groceries. I felt so alone
that I forgot my anger for a moment and was sorry I hadn't
set something up with Franny. I wanted to call her and say,
"Hey, let's get together right now. Let's go to the beach and
work on our tans and gossip about men. Let's try to locate
something decent to smoke. Let's go to the Grove and drum
up some action."*

*But I had to straighten up the house and do the laundry
and after that I had promised to take the kids to a movie. By
evening I would be tired, and I would still have to go through
my mail, pay some bills, iron clothes for the workweek, and
try to get to bed early. I couldn't afford to screw around and
act like a complete flake. So I didn't call Franny, and I
didn't really feel hostile anymore, because I realized that it
wasn't pride or anger that had kept me from calling her all
those months. It was just that I had changed and I didn't
want to see her anymore.*

SIDE TWO

*I ran into Bonnie at the supermarket. It was really embar-
rassing. I felt guilty as hell for not calling in so long. She
looked awful, worse than when Bob was sick. That girl has
got to get out and start having some fun.*

*And I had so much to tell her. I wanted to tell her all
about my new boyfriend and about my trip to Europe and
about the new job. But she put up this wall the minute she
saw me, this great wall of sorrow, so I just took off. I'd love
to have said, "Hey, Bonnie, let's go to the beach. I'll tell you
about him. Let's have some laughs about all the craziness.
Come on. Let's go." I'd have loved to say that, but she's
gotten so negative. She is so into her own problems that it
makes me feel guilty for just being happy. And I don't need*

that aggravation. I really don't need it because most of the time I am right on the borderline of depression myself. I don't need to be reminded that life sucks. I don't need that aggravation.

Oh, God, she's in the next checkout line. Boy, if looks could kill. I don't understand what happened. We used to be such good friends. She used to be so much fun and up for anything, even when Bob was sick. I'd give anything to be able to call her and talk like we used to, but I don't want to sit and listen to her bitch, for Christ's sake. And to tell the truth, she really doesn't have it so bad. She has a good job and good kids. She has it better than a lot of people I know. If she could just see that, it would be one thing. But all she does is feel sorry for herself, yap about her "bad karma" and her "rotten deal" and how tired she is all the time. So why should I call her and feel useless about everything and end up getting depressed too? I'm sorry, but I don't want to anymore.

Neither of us wanted to anymore. It wasn't worth it. She seemed too flaky and I seemed too negative. We no longer complemented each other. We didn't feel "hey, I'm terrific" when we got together. Most of the friendships we make are narcissistic relationships. We look for what we think is a flattering reflection of ourselves in the people we spend time with. We admire the qualities that we would like to absorb into our own definition. These friendships perish like flowers when the weather changes. And it is not so much their change itself that bothers us. Our own reflection is the problem. It comes back at an unfamiliar angle and presents an image that just may not be welcome anymore.

When Bob was alive we seemed to have a lot of single friends like Franny. They were entertaining. They had funny stories and interesting sex lives and a welcome absence of marital problems. We bounced off of them and didn't quite feel like the old married couple we had become. After Bob died I found myself drawn to the couples I knew. I'd get antsy at night. My kids went to bed at nine-thirty, and after that I was lost. My family felt incomplete. If I pedaled over to a couple's house in the neighborhood, I could talk to a marriage for an hour before bedtime. I needed to catch a glimpse of that domestic reflection of myself. It was comforting and familiar and certainly a lot healthier than Valium. They would be glad to see me. They would unbolt their door, usher me in, shut off the TV, and bring out some wine. Their first question wouldn't be "How are you managing?" or "How are the kids?" It would be "How's your sex life?"

The tables had turned. I felt obligated to answer and to entertain. It was a fair exchange. I needed the hominess and they needed the cheap entertainment. Just give her a glass of wine and she'll babble for hours. She'll tell it all and if there's nothing to tell, she'll make something up. She's better than "Dallas."

"My trip to the islands was great," I'd say. "I did some sailing and got quite a bit of writing done."

"Any men?" they'd ask.

"Well, there was this one neat guy, sort of tough, with a big boat. He showed up at my room one night with a bag of ropes. See, he wanted me to tie him up."

"Oh, God, no! You didn't, you didn't. Did you?"

"Well, you know . . . I *was* on vacation."

A single woman doesn't usually last long in a pack of couples, and my track record turned out to be pretty grim. I was either an extra—"Gee, Bonnie, we invited some couples over for dinner tonight. Why don't you stop by later for dessert"—or I was a threat. If a marriage was at all shaky, a case began to build against my presence. It built up after hours, after the jokes and the wine and the good times. It built up until I found myself totally cut off. I was cut off for all the little misdemeanors that occur in any friendship and that don't add up unless someone is looking for an out. I'd try to iron things out, but the case had been closed and the verdict delivered.

"Joan sees you as a threat," he'd say. "You have to admit, there was some electricity between us."

I looked at him in surprise. I didn't know what he was talking about. He was my pal. I thought we had all been great friends, but I was wrong. As long as Bob was around and I was part of a pair, I had remained neutralized. Without him I was voracious, I generated electricity, I confused the chemistry, I was a threat. And it helped them to be able to see me as a bad person. It restored their sense of order and justice. Look at what happened. Her husband died. How could that happen to someone who was innocent? She must be up to no good. She must be looking to make trouble between us.

The absolute opposite was true. I didn't want to screw up anything. I wanted the couple together, fat and happy, so I could snuggle up to a relationship and hold on to it like a teddy bear. A door shut. There was no methadone marriage available to ease my addiction to the state of matrimony, and I was meticulously pecked out of the flock of couples.

I really needed company. I had always lived with another voice and it was difficult to be without one. I needed some response to make me feel certain that I was still there. I needed a sympathetic ear, and it occurred to me that I wasn't alone in this. There were plenty of women in the same situation. In fact, every other woman I knew was single and they all seemed to be able to do it. They could all get through the day, the evening, the night, without banging on a couple's door, demanding a fix of some remembered warmth. Maybe they could teach me something.

I called up Angela. We had never been close friends, but after Bob died she had stopped by a few times to see how I was doing, and she always seemed kind and together. We made plans to see a movie. She had been happy to hear from me, but by the time she came by her mood was oppressive. There had been an encounter with her ex-husband.

"You're lucky Bob died," she opened as I got into her car. "I wish to God that Sam had died." It began to rain. She accelerated her car and switched on the wipers. They snapped across the surface of the windshield, skimming off the droplets that pelted the glass. "I would like to get myself a little gun, and put it to his head right there," she continued, pointing to her scrubbed, powdered, perfumed temple. "And then I would like to just pull that little trigger and—pow."

After the movie she needed cigarettes and found a convenience store in the neighborhood. She pulled carelessly into the crowded lot and parked in the loading zone. I waited in the car for her, surrounded by an assortment of gas guzzlers that had been salvaged from the 1960s. Spanish music was blaring from one of the heaps attracting a group of young men. It was Saturday night in "Little Havana."

Angela returned to the car, tamping the pack of cigarettes against her fist. She backed up and smashed into an automobile that had parked behind us. The young men looked up from their music. She calmly lit a cigarette, pulled up, and then backed into the car again, hitting it harder. The men began to move toward us. She inched forward, shifted into reverse, and rammed the car once more.

"Jesus, Angela, what are you doing? Let's get out of here."

I was really scared. Someone had been shot a few days earlier for merely honking at a Latin driver, and there we were, on their turf, deliberately bashing this flagrantly Cuban car over and over again. I expected at least a round of machine-gun fire and a Molotov cocktail.

"Shall we stop somewhere for a drink?" she asked.

"No, thanks. I just want to go home."

She drove me back home. Fear was crawling all over me. I was afraid they were following us. I was afraid she would crash. I was afraid she would look for another confrontation. But my biggest fear was of the bitterness that can overpower anyone who feels alone and deadened emotionally. It frightened me because I had begun to feel cut off from any real understanding and generosity. It frightened me because I had begun to taste bitterness when I thought about my situation. Bob was dead and most of my friendships were dead too.

There is an obscure Jewish saying that a man should do two things in his life—find a teacher and buy a friend. When I first heard this phrase, the "buy a friend" part struck me as being a bit odd. And because it was such unexpected advice, it attracted my attention and got me to think it through a little further. You didn't buy your friends, but a friendship did have to be worked at. Friends didn't just happen without an exchange of action and time, and what was buying but an exchange of one valuable for another. I felt deserted by my old friends, but I had made no effort to see them. Maybe they felt just as deserted by me. Somehow I had to begin making time for the few people I really cared about. I had to give as much to my friends as I expected from them.

And I really expected a lot. I expected more than companionship. I needed an extraordinary amount of support. Friendship had become a necessity. I had lost my identity. I was the detective, hot on the trail of a missing person, and I needed help from the people who had been close. They could give me leads and clues about the nature and whereabouts of that missing person.

15

Sometimes I go to bed and I am amazed at how warm and good it is possible to feel. Sometimes I go to bed and wish that I could wake up and be something else, something sensible—like a nun. The necessity of dealing with my sexuality put me onto an emotional roller coaster. I was up, down, confused, exhilarated, scared shitless, and ready for more. I felt that I was just the right age for it, or that I was much too old for it, or that I would always be too young for it.

I was ambivalent because I was confused. This wasn't something I had planned to do. At thirty-five I had expected the comfortable intimacy that comes, for better or for worse, with fifteen years of marriage. My life had been planned and plotted out so neatly that I could flip through the future as if it were a Triptik.

> Miles 35–40: For the most part a quiet and familiar trip. Some confusion at 36 as sons reach maturity. Stay on the well-trodden route. A scenic detour at 38 may be necessary to break the monotony of the journey, but return to

the thoroughfare by marker 39. Prepare for a major road-
block as husband reaches 40.

I certainly hadn't planned to be driving through the moral
wasteland of the 1980s without my best buddy, without my
bodyguard. But there I was, barreling along in the fast lane,
chucking the guide out the window, and to complicate matters, I had three kids in the backseat.

I met a lot of men cruising at 30,000 feet, strapped into a
seat and sipping a screwdriver with a couple of vodka min-
iatures lined up like soldiers on my tray. He would be seated
next to me by chance, and we would enjoy a fast relationship. It stayed verbal and congenial because we were both
battened down, blocked in between an armrest and a tray
table, with a few hours to kill. The encounter would trail off
as the wheels clunked down, the no-smoking sign lit up, the
stewardess snatched our glasses, and we descended to
earth.

These were my warm-ups, my dress rehearsals. I had
their undivided attention. They were mine for the duration
of the flight. The only possible competition was a briefcase
or a Sony Walkman. I spent a two-and-a-half-hour trip to
New York in the company of a perfect Prussian who manu-
factured tanks, and a two-hour trip from Charlotte shooting
the breeze with a cocaine dealer who started his career
hawking moonshine. I had a chance to practice my lines and
listen to theirs. There was a new stand in every trip, and it
was perfectly safe, because when the plane landed we both
had to slip off in our own directions.

I learned a lot about a man in the course of a flight. There
are no secrets necessary at 30,000 feet. They talked about
business or travel or women, but it was the dialogues about
women that really caught me and stuck in my mind. I grew
alert for an indication of what men wanted in a woman. It
has definitely changed since we were all teens or in our

twenties, and I was lucky to have had the chance to check the direction of the wind before pushing off from shore.

"My wife left me about three years ago. She was having an affair with some low life, and then she took off with him. I don't really miss her. No, she got to be a real pain in the ass, and it's actually been a relief to have her gone. But I miss the body. I just miss having a warm body."

"I'm happily married. I love my wife, I really do, and I wouldn't do anything in the world to hurt her. She's such a sweet thing. She really doesn't deserve that. But I enjoy other women too, and I really believe that the affairs I've had have actually helped my marriage. You see, when I have someone else, she's a lot easier to take. She doesn't annoy me so much. She's less of a bitch."

"I was divorced and lived alone for two years, and boy, it was really ruining my health—all the drinking and running around. Boy, I'll tell you. So I got married again last month —for health reasons, you understand."

"I've been divorced twice. The first one I married because I had to and, of course, that didn't work out at all. The second one I married because I was in love and that didn't work out either. So now I figure if you have your health, and if you have enough money to buy whatever you want, and if you have someone to screw when you need it, you've got it all. There just ain't no more, honey, there just ain't no more."

"You want a black beauty? I got black beauties. I got coke and Quaaludes too. You want a Quaalude? I need a place to crash in Miami. You got a boyfriend? You sure you don't want a Quaalude? How about a kiss? You look like you could use a kiss. You want a kiss?"

On a trip from Detroit I had the opportunity to sit next to a real professional. I noticed him on the flight going up in the morning. He sat across from me and was totally engrossed in the contents of his briefcase. He gnawed annoyingly on his pencil as he shuffled through his papers. I arrived in Detroit at 11:30, did my work, and was ready to leave on the 6:20 back to Miami. He was waiting in the holdroom for the same flight.

"Oh, hello," I said as I boarded the plane. He was seated next to me. "Weren't you on the flight up this morning?"

"Yes" was all he said. As soon as we were in the sky he pulled down his tray, opened his briefcase, pulled out his papers and began jotting down notes, shuffling pages and gnawing on his pencil.

The 6:20 from Detroit is a dinner flight on a 727. In coach it's three tedious hours strapped into a narrow seat, fighting with the adjacent passenger for the rights to the armrest, and trying to eat a tasteless meal coughed out of a warmer.

In first class it's happy hour all the way. The stewardess urges you to take drink after drink. She gives you two at a time in between a service of salad and steak, hot fudge sundaes and after-dinner liqueurs. By the time the plane reaches Miami, the entire first class is crocked.

Except for the guy sitting next to me, who refused drink after drink and his entire meal service. The passengers around us were getting increasingly louder and lewder as he worked. The lady across the aisle staggered to her feet and grabbed the stack of papers that covered his tray.

"What are you working on? I wanna see."

He grabbed the papers back and pulled them from her. Then he pushed the woman and she fell into her seat as he stuck the papers into his briefcase, slammed it shut and locked it. The drunk lady was back on her feet when the stewardess came to establish order.

"Please sit down, miss, and keep your seat belt secure. Let the gentleman work. Would you like another drink?"

"Oh, I love you." She threw her arms around the stewardess. "I love all the old ones. Gimme another scotch and soda."

The stewardess shook herself free, apologized to the man and went to get more booze. Everything calmed down except for me. I was on my toes. I was curious.

"What business are you in?" I asked the man next to me.

"Accounting," he snapped. He kept his eyes on the woman across the aisle until she began molesting the man next to her. Feeling safe, he opened his briefcase, pulled out his papers, and carefully arranged them on his tray.

Accounting my ass, I thought. This guy doesn't even have a calculator. I sat perfectly still and let my neck stretch in the direction of his seat. I focused my eyes on the report he was laboring over and scanned it for numbers. It looked more like an application than a financial sheet. The title was all in capital letters and easiest to read. My neck stretched a bit more and the title came into focus. It read: *The Second and Final Wife of Phillip Cornell.*

I sat back in amazement. He's an assassin, I thought. The man was so totally involved in making notes on his report that he didn't notice me edging closer to read the entire sheet.

The Second and Final Wife of Phillip Cornell
The object of this search is to find a suitable partner for the client. The requirements for such a partner are listed below. Any woman considered must satisfy all requirements.
1. Age: 26–35
2. Height: 5'3"–5'5"
3. Weight: 115–126
4. Build: slim without being overly athletic

5. Coloring: fair skin, dark hair acceptable
6. Facial features: Anglican
7. Interests: tennis, bridge, charitable organizations
8. Personality type: passively social

I stopped reading after item 8. So that was what they wanted. Here was a man—Phillip Cornell—with the resources to hire his own private matchmaker to scour the states for a suitable mate, an ideal woman, and he wanted passively social. Mr. Cornell, who could have anything he wanted served to him on a silver platter, wanted Velveeta cheese on white bread.

As the pilot announced the beginning of our descent to the Miami airport, the stewardess asked if I wanted one more drink before she closed the bar. I took a double.

When I got home and told Peach the story, he asked me why I didn't hand in an application.

"You had a real 'in,' a contact. Boy, you really missed your chance. It sounds like a great job. Why didn't you apply?"

"Are you kidding? Passively social? I couldn't afford the lobotomy."

They knew too much. They were all twenty years older and they knew too much. They knew how hard it was to make anything work out. They had wanted to love and be loved back, but had ended up hurting someone or getting hurt and trying again. In the end they were still alone. So, what the heck, why not go for something possible, something easy, like a warm body or a place to crash or someone passively social.

And what did I want? Ms. Goody Two-Shoes, who had never been hatcheted by a divorce, who had not watched the dream turn into a nightmare of bitterness, laid claim to a more inspired set of requirements than Mr. Cornell had. But although she claimed to be looking for another serious steak-and-potatoes relationship, when the buffet opened she went straight for the cheesecake.

He stood out like a green light. I spotted him the minute I walked into his club in New York with my friend whose ex-husband was his accountant. He was leaning against the bar with a glass of vodka in one hand and an Oriental woman in the other. He looked perfect—perfectly tall, perfectly blond, perfectly groomed, perfectly dressed, and perfectly high. The great Jay. A perfect "go."

God, I thought, give me this man for one night and I'll believe in you.

So when my friend called a few months later to tell me that Jay was in Florida with her ex-husband, and wondered if I would join them for dinner, I said yes, dumped the kids with Peach, got dressed, and was ready and pacing a half hour early.

I talked too much at dinner. He laughed at everything I said and talked even more than I did. "Hey, I know I'm babbling. Don't pay any attention to me, Toots, because I'm totally nuts. I've been in the saloon business too long. My brain is disintegrating. Have some more wine." He caught the waiter's eye and said, "Whiskey for my women. Drugs for my horses. Normal."

After dinner we all walked to my friend's car.

"Do you have to get home now?" he asked before I got in. "I could drive you in a while if you want to stay."

Peach was with the kids, so I told my friend and her ex-husband to go, and I went back with Jay to his apartment. He spent the rest of the evening telling me outrageous stories about himself. He could have made the *Guinness Book of World Records* with a single act. And I was charmed. It was a riot. There I sat on a Knoll couch, my drink on a

Breuton table, listening to this incredibly classy man tell me how in a state of total inebriation he had once collected frozen dog turds from the front of his building and had locked them in his mailbox, how he had woken up in his bed with two women, a man and a chicken, and how he had gotten so drunk before coming to Florida that the only way he could board the plane was to get on his hands and knees and crawl down the loading bridge.

Peach was still up when Jay drove me home. He had some friends over. We could see them moving around in the living room through the window.

"Shall I come in," he asked, "or will this be awkward?"

"Of course you can come in. It's my house. He's the live-in baby-sitter. It won't be awkward."

"Are you sleeping with him?"

"No."

"Is he a fag?"

"No, he's an unemployed writer."

He came in and walked through my house taking in my paintings, my sculptures, the pile of dishes in the sink. He talked with Pete for a while and looked him over. He seemed amused by everything. "He's not a fag," Jay said. "I thought you were even nuttier than me. I thought you were leaving your kids with a faggot, but that guy is no fag."

And then he took my hand. "Listen, do me one favor, Toots. Promise me one thing. When you get rich and famous, and they ask you to show your paintings in the Whitney, promise me you'll say no. Because your paintings are really shitty. I'm sorry, but they're just awful. Now, what do you have? Do you have any booze? Do you have any drugs?"

I poured him a glass of vodka. "I have a whole lot of Demerol left from when Bob was sick," I offered. "'Would you like some of that?"

He closed his eyes. When he opened them again he looked so awfully sad and I was sorry I had said that, but I always thought that my paintings were pretty good. "Normal," he said, which I took as a yes and I went up to my room to find the Demerol.

He followed me upstairs, closed the door, and put down his drink. Then he took off all his clothes and got into my bed. I was surprised. It seemed a little sudden, but, hey, what did I know? This man's been around. He knows what he's doing. You wanted to dance, now follow the lead. It's easy—a two-step.

"It'll all come back," Eileen had said, *"like riding a bike."*

"That's my side," I said.

"Oh, sorry, Toots." He moved over and I took off my clothes and slid in next to him.

He was the green light and that seemed to be what I was looking for. Nothing too deep—just a green light, green for go.

Red lights aren't as easy. Who ever says no anymore? It is an act of treason, an aggressively reactionary step in the sexual revolution. If you say no you are possibly a lesbian or have an outbreak of herpes. Saying no is almost obscene.

I should have said no to dinner. I had gone out with him before. I knew that I didn't want to go to bed with him, so I could have said no when he asked me to dinner. But he was intelligent and fun to talk to, and I said yes. And then, like a jerk, I said yes to listening to some tapes and that brought me up to his room and to the next yes.

Which was where I faltered. He was a nice, attractive man and I had enjoyed the evening. So why was I eyeing the door, trying to think of an exit line? What was wrong with me? Sex was a terrific thing. I just needed to relax a little. It would be awful. I didn't want him. What was I doing there? How could I get out? Maybe I was nuts and it would really be great. How could I tell if I didn't give it a try? Nobody would get hurt if I said yes. It would be so easy. Just another glass of wine and I'd be on tilt anyway.

"No." God, did I really say that? "No, I'm not going to stay. Thank you for dinner. It was nice. Good-bye."

He didn't walk me down to my car. I didn't care. I felt strangely secure. I felt as if someone really cared about me. I put on my seat belt for the first time and carefully drove myself home.

My brother Jerry wasn't amused when I told him that a man I was seeing turned out to have a wife. But because he is a psychiatrist and because I brought it up, he laid the guilt on me. "Why do you think you are always getting involved in these no-win relationships?"

"Gee, I don't know, Jerry. I never thought of it like that. All the interesting men I meet end up being out of the question for one reason or another. But I don't think I look for trouble. These guys just find me. Anyway, that's all there is. Anybody that makes sense is already taken."

There was a long pause, a long long-distance pause on the telephone that said one thing—"Bullshit."

"Well, how are the kids?" He switched the conversation to something we could talk about easily, and we did, but he sounded worried when we said good-bye. He had planted a time bomb in my mind and was waiting for it to go off. The kids had been a safe subject but if I thought about them long enough I always got back to the issue of men. The kids were there in the backseat wherever I went, whatever detour or dead-end street I decided to turn down. They were there watching the scenery, trusting me, and making me feel guilty as hell. In the back of my mind, in the back of everybody's mind, they needed a father, and that didn't seem to be the kind of action Mommy was drumming up.

"You can get married again, Mom," Miles said. "Don't let us stand in your way. You've got to think about yourself."

There wasn't any realistic candidate to even consider when he announced this. He was really saying, "Why don't you get married again? What's standing in your way? Think about us."

There was one big thing standing in my way. I didn't know what I wanted anymore. I had changed so much since Bob died that if it had all been a colossal mistake and he walked through the door, plunked down his briefcase and looked around carefully, he would probably ask me for two things —a gin and tonic and a divorce.

The house would be a mess. Dinner would be sitting soggy in a Kentucky Fried Chicken box, and I would be dressed to the hilt, yelling the evening's commands like a drill sergeant —"Miles, bring in the laundry. Seth, do the dishes. Asher, walk the dog." Then I would hand the situation over to him, excuse myself, and rush to the airport for the night flight to New York.

I didn't need the same things anymore. When I lost the keystone of my household and I reassembled the structure, every piece needed a new position so it could stand. I didn't need a man to take care of me. I didn't need a house to fuss over. I didn't need three little princes to pick up after. But what I did need was still unclear to me.

"You better make sure that you go after what you really need," an old friend said as she packed up the pieces of her second marriage. "Because as sure as anything, you're going to get what you go looking for, and if you're not careful, if you're not honest—oh, boy. You could end up with something that doesn't make you happy."

I had to call Jerry back and tell him not to worry, that it was all okay. There was something safe about a no-win relationship. If I didn't play to win, I couldn't really lose. No one could let me down. No one could divorce me or die on me. I needed time. I needed to stall for a while and figure out who I was becoming and what that meant.

I wasn't without needs, not by a long shot. There was a screaming need in my life for something, and maybe that's what scared some sense into me. I was confused. I was vulnerable. It was no time for making decisions or for anything serious. It was time for more sail. Forget the keel. Forget holding things on course. I could be the sail and have more sail too, and that just meant I had to go where the wind took me. I could only run with the wind. So the men I liked, the no-win relationships, were exactly what I needed. I wasn't ready to plot a course. Not yet. I was flying downwind with as much sail as I could carry.

PART FOUR

16

Fading Rainbow was published a year to the day after Bob's death. When my editor asked if I would be interested in doing a publicity tour to promote the book, I said yes without hesitation.

"It's great exposure. There's no advertising we can buy to match seven minutes of TV time. But it could be a drag. You'll have to fly into strange cities and find your way to radio and TV stations where you'll be asked personal questions by strangers who probably haven't even read the book. You'll have to answer the same questions with a sense of freshness, and, Bonnie, don't forget, it may bring up a lot of depressing memories. So think about it."

"I'll do it," I said.

"Well, write me a bio and we'll see what kind of response we get."

We got three yeses and one maybe. The yeses were from morning talk shows in St. Louis, Cleveland, and Philadelphia. The maybe was from "Good Morning America."

"Why didn't you tell them about me?" Miles whined.

"This could be my big chance. Didn't you tell them I went to the Coconut Grove Children's Theatre and can act and sing? I can even tap dance a little. Maybe I'll be discovered. I can't *believe* you didn't tell them about me."

I couldn't believe it when I did. My editor loved the idea and so did the people at "Good Morning America." A death, a book, a widow, and now she's throwing in a kid. Who could resist? A short tour was arranged, and I took some time off from work to do it. I was excited. I had never been on TV before.

"Figure out a few things that you want to say," my editor advised, "then get around to saying them no matter what they ask. Don't let the conversation drag. Keep the ball moving. Try to think of what you could say about yourself that will interest people in reading Bob's book."

I didn't think at all about what I wanted to say. I thought about what I wanted to wear but not what I would say. I didn't realize what I had gotten myself into.

The first show I did was in St. Louis, which is my hometown. My mother was waiting for me at the airport, but she was so nervous that we had to call my sister Eileen to drive us to the station. The old buildings looked familiar, but the route downtown had changed. Innerbelts and interstates had shredded the city I used to know.

We arrived at the station fifteen minutes early and I was introduced to the man who would conduct the interview. There was something familiar about him, but I couldn't place it. Eileen gave me hints.

"Kiddy show . . . cartoons . . . after 'Captain Kangaroo.' "

"My God," I realized, "I'm going to be interviewed by Corky the Clown." I was to be the second guest. The first was a tall, emaciated woman dressed in a miniskirt and a sleeveless jacket. Her face was lost beneath a mask of makeup. Her hair had been hacked off and tipped turquoise to boot. The topic of her segment was "dressing for success."

She began a harangue on the state of feminine fashion that led up to her thesis. She felt that women had trouble in the business world because they were not comfortable with what they wore. She thought that women would feel much more self-confident and would be much more effective and successful if they would stop wearing underwear altogether and just wear pantyhose.

Corky could keep a straight face. He was a pro. I couldn't. "Mom," I whispered, "do you suppose I have time to slip off my panties before this interview? I don't want anything to stand in the way of success."

"Shhh."

"I can't follow this act with a dead husband."

"Shhh."

"Oh, shit. Oh, shit. It's a commercial. I'm next."

The producer began counting down. I took my seat in the mock living room next to Corky. The lights flashed on. The air in the studio was ice cold. I was introduced to a camera.

"How did you feel when you found out your husband had a terminal illness?" the ex-clown asked.

Just like that. No pussyfooting around. Right to the point. After all, I wasn't there for my looks. I wasn't there for my taste in clothes. I was there because I had witnessed a death and experienced a personal loss and because I had been nuts enough to say yes to talking about it on television.

Let's see, Corky, how did I feel. . . . I thought about jumping up and screaming and cursing and breaking one of the ceramic lamps over the plastic-laminate table. I thought that might approach an accurate description of how I had felt.

"Well," I said instead, "I was in shock at first and then I

was angry and depressed, and then I got on with my life and with preparing myself somehow for what would happen."

"How can you prepare yourself for something like that?" he asked.

By drinking much more vodka, I thought, by trying to overdose on obligations, by sleeping fourteen hours a day.

"Well, you can't really prepare yourself emotionally," I said, "but if you can prepare yourself economically, that's just one less problem you'll have to deal with." God, I sound like a frigging insurance salesman.

The cameras rolled around me like cyclopes. The minutes were whittled away by the questions and the answers. Was I saying anything? Was I making any sense? Was I boring?

As unceremoniously as it began, the segment ended. Corky thanked me for coming and I thanked him for something. The next segment was on tape, so we sat around and talked for a while.

"I really prefer doing kids' shows," he admitted. "I'll go back to it when we move to our new studio. There's no room here for a live audience, and kids' shows are no fun without the kids."

He ended up telling me about how hard it was for him to accept a recent death in his family. He seemed relieved to have someone to talk to about it, even for a few minutes, sitting on a dime-store couch in an ice-cold television set. He had been hurt and he had felt a loss, and there hadn't been many people he could say that to.

My next stop was Cleveland. The studio there was a three-ring circus. The camera crew lugged equipment from the live news set to the live commercial set to the talk show set. If they weren't quick enough to make a shot, the producer moaned, cursed, and dropped a sequence. All the guests for the talk show sat against the wall on folding chairs, watching in amazement. Nobody knew when they were on except the producer, who scurried over every few minutes to point to one of us and say, "You."

"I promote gay cops in San Francisco," the man on the folding chair next to me confided. "What's your shtick?"

"Well," I answered, "I wish I could say I had something gay to promote, but actually I'm promoting a book. It's about dying. My husband had leukemia and was writing a book about it. But he died before it was done, so I finished it. Now I'm doing a promotion tour."

"You know," he said, "we have something in common. We're both dealing with topics that are coming out of the closet—sexuality and death."

I did my shtick right after he did his. I had two seven-minute segments. The first was a series of questions similar to the ones asked me in St. Louis. During the second, I was to answer telephone calls.

"I just want to know what you have that I don't have," the amplified voice demanded. "My husband died a year ago and I'm still not over it. And I'm a good Christian."

Was I over it? I hadn't noticed. Was she right? If that was it, how come I still have this creepy sense of unreality? How come I still feel so incomplete?

"Well," I answered the camera with the blinking red light, "what has helped me is having the kids and a job. I have to get up every morning and get them going. I have to function. Commitments help. Friends and family help and taking time to do the things you always enjoyed help, too."

God, I make it sound so simple, so inane. I have reduced grief to the level of a television commercial. Here it is, folks, the amazing one-step grieving process. Just focus on yourself, and—snap—your life is in order.

I felt like a fraud. The phone calls were serious. The questions deserved to be answered honestly, and all I was able to do was look the camera straight in the lens and lie by omission, because I was on morning television, because there were only a few minutes to talk, and because the four-letter feelings were simply not allowed.

They had a live audience waiting for me in Philadelphia. I didn't think that would make a difference but it did.

"How did your children react when you finally told them that Bob had a terminal disease?"

Now that was a new one. Nobody had dared ask me about the kids yet. How did they react? Could I pass? Could I say, "What kids"? Could I say, "You got the wrong lady"?

"They didn't believe it," I said. I could see the rows of eyes beyond the cameras. I was talking to people, not just to a camera. I started to shake. "They saw their father running three miles a day and going to work . . . uh, they believed doctors could cure things . . . uh, we all, uh, thought he had ten years then and uh, you know, ten years is a lifetime to a . . . uh, ten-year-old." I shook through the rest of the interview. I was shaking when it was over and the producer approached me and asked if I would take some calls that were too personal to put on the air.

The live audience gave me a collective sad stare as I walked past. A widow with the shakes. Bring on the dancing girls. Two hold lights blinked at me from the phone. I pushed down on one and picked up the receiver.

"My husband died a few months ago," the voice began, "and I still communicate with him. Is that normal? I mean, I know he's dead, but sometimes he really seems to be there and I talk things over with him and it makes me feel better. Is that crazy?"

"No," I said, "I don't think that's crazy. I mean, just because someone is gone physically, doesn't mean they're totally severed from your memory. How could they be? Sometimes I have an experience and imagine how Bob would have related to it. Sometimes that shades my reactions. There are times when I feel he's with me more than other times. Sometimes he's sitting right on my shoulder. I think that's normal. I think it would be crazy if we felt totally cut off from someone we were close to for so many years."

By the time I pushed the second blinking button, my shaking had stopped.

"I have the same disease your husband had," the voice said, "and I just want to know if there was much pain at the end."

Pain. Physical pain was bad enough, but how could I evaluate the amount of pain there is in watching yourself fade, cell by cell, thought by thought, color by color? How could I evaluate the pain of knowing you would never see your kids grow into adulthood? I wanted to hold that voice on the phone. Did he have a wife? Did he have kids? Could I possibly say anything that would give him courage?

"No, it was more weakness than actual physical pain. In fact, that last night, when he got pneumonia, there had been no pain medication on his chart in such a long time that they had to call a doctor to enter a prescription."

He thanked me and said good-bye. I put down the receiver and slipped out of the studio.

My editor called the next day. "Something came up. The 'Good Morning America' date has been changed," she said. "They want to do it a few weeks later. I know that Miles will be in camp, but they'll fly him down, and you can meet him in New York. David Hartman will do the interview. It will be on July third."

"July third! You know that I planned to go on vacation that week with my sister. Can't it be this week or the week after the Fourth of July?"

"David Hartman's on vacation this week and the week after the Fourth gets you into the preparations for the Republican Convention."

"Listen," I argued, "I need this vacation, and these shows are just killing me. I don't think book sales are up. I can't seem to interest people in the book. My friends aren't even buying it. And I'm an absolute wreck."

There was a long silence on the phone. She was wondering if I would back out and let her down, if I would choose a week in St. Maarten with my sister over seven minutes with David Hartman.

"Okay, I'll do it."

"Thanks," she said.

"But I'm not convinced this tour is helping sales at all. I feel like I'm just subjecting myself to this public ordeal for nothing."

"It's not for nothing."

"Will 'Good Morning America' help?"

"It can't hurt."

She called the next day. "You're going to kill me. The show has been changed to the ninth, maybe the tenth."

I called my sister and we rescheduled our vacation. The day before I left I got the final date—the eighth.

There were two flights out of St. Maarten on the seventh of July. The first one was full and the second had been cancelled. It was every pass rider's nightmare—a commitment thousands of miles away and not one available seat. And then I spotted them—three tall men stretching their legs and picking up some duty-free cigarettes. The three great white gods in black suits strolling through the St. Maarten airport could only be one thing. They could only be the pilots.

I introduced myself and explained my problem. "Could you do me a favor and let me sit in the jump seat? I'm not really authorized, but I sometimes work on designing ramp facilities, and I'll never get out of here in time if you don't help me."

"Well, we're not supposed to," the captain said, "but . . . what the heck. Let's do her a favor. What the heck."

I grabbed my suitcase and followed them out to the ramp and up to the cockpit. They strapped me into the jump seat.

"One thing," the flight engineer said, "one thing you've got to do, see, 'cause you're not supposed to be up here. Now, if we start to crash would you do us a favor so we don't end up looking bad? Would you please be sure to crawl out of here and die in first class?"

I promised I would. They began the procedure that would get us into the air. The flight engineer chanted off a list of checks and the copilot read responsively from the gauges in front of him. They consecrated every gauge, lever, and dial, and then the chanting stopped. Amen. We were ready to fly.

It was the best seat in the house. I was surrounded by the sky, and the sea spread out like a blanket below me. I was on my way. I could finally relax. Three shows down and one to go. I didn't think that I was selling many books, but I knew that my editor had been right when she said, "It's not for nothing."

A year had passed. When Bob died I didn't think that time would pass, but it had. Minutes at first and then days that turned into months and finally a whole year had gone by. I was talking about it. I was talking about it to strangers, to cameras, and to voices on the phone, but most important of all, I was talking about it to myself.

I was gaining a perspective on what had happened. It was like getting up in the air and looking down at the landscape. The relationship of one place to another became obvious. On the ground the immediate area was all that seemed to exist. But from the sky a spot became a patch in the whole fabric. This didn't make the spot any less important. It just put it into context. Which is what I began to do when I started promoting Bob's book.

"What did you say?" "How did you feel?" "What about the kids?" "Do you still miss him?" "What did you do?"

What had I done? I had cut a path through shock, confusion, anger, and guilt from Bob's death to where I sat right then. I had a past. His death was a part of it and so were all the right, wrong, half-assed, inspired, and desperate steps that had followed.

We were waiting for David Hartman to finish up with Julia Child and her string beans. I glanced over at Miles, who was sitting next to me on the "Good Morning America" couch. His legs were crossed, his fists were clenched, and he looked clammy underneath the makeup. I uncrossed his legs and shook out his hands and told him to relax.

David Hartman lumbered across the set during the commercial. He slouched into his seat.

"Hi, I'm David Hartman," he said. "Thanks for coming and sharing your story with us this morning."

The cameras rolled over. A last-minute adjustment was made to my mike and then we were on. Miles stole the show.

"What did you think when you read your father's book?" David asked.

"It made me sad to read about the hospital and the tests, because some of the tests were painful. My favorite parts were the parts about running. My father loved to run. I never went because—well, because I'm lazy. But my father loved the running and nature. He really loved nature. He would run and stop and squeeze some sea grapes and just feel the juice run down his arm."

"What do you remember most about your father? What kinds of things did you talk about with him?"

"We talked about a lot of things, like what college I should go to and about death. The talks about death really stand out in my mind. I think everybody should think about dying. It's really crazy that people don't, because we all have to experience death at least once in our lives."

I had gone to the cemetery a few weeks before. The empty grass that had once spread out alongside Bob's grave was filled up with markers and mounds of earth. Each marker meant that there had been a death in a family. It was sad. It was part of the bargain.

"Well, we know how Miles is doing," said David Hartman. The cameras took their cue and turned on me. "But how are you doing, Bonnie? How has your life changed in the year since Bob died?"

"Really, just about everything has changed," I said. "When you live with someone for a long time, so much of your action and responses are a balance to theirs. When they're gone, there's this big gap you have to fill. You have to fill it with regard to your family and your friends and yourself. Just about everything has changed since Bob died."

When the segment was over, David Hartman asked us to wait on the set while he did the sign-off.

"You know," he said when he returned, "I read Bob's book last night and I didn't see how you could say anything in the confines of 'Good Morning America' to really do it justice. But I think that Miles did just that." Then he talked for a while about the memories he had of his father. We all have to experience death at least once in our lives.

17

I faced a room full of widows. They kept coming in and filling up the seats in the large classroom at the YWCA. I was surprised at the turnout. I still felt a little uncomfortable with my marital status. I still felt as though it singled me out as a loser. I remembered the first time I had to check that little box next to the word "widow." It was on a dental form. Seth had to get a tooth filled, and I had to admit to an insurance company that I was indeed a widow. There were about seventy women in front of me, and each one had filled in an application, written out a check, and put on a name tag to be there as a widow.

A group called the Displaced Homemakers was sponsoring the forum. It was to be a workshop for women in transition, for wives with "late" husbands, for widows. I had agreed to speak about change and balance.

I delivered a short speech and I had the devout attention of every displaced homemaker in the room. The speakers after me were widows or therapists or both. Their topics were "The Grief and the Bereavement Process," "Women and Money," "Old Friends/New Friends," and "What Happens to Your Sexuality." The speeches could have gone on for days. Not a single woman would have left her seat, not even the little Chinese woman who barely spoke English but understood that her feelings of desperation were finally being addressed.

We were coming out of the closet. We were coming together to talk about our grief, our sense of identity, our loneliness, our ability to cope, our sexuality, and about the painful progression from wife to widow and back to woman. The speeches were good, but the questions they provoked were better. They were the questions of women who had probably never questioned anything before, because everything had always been just right. And then something happened and things weren't just right anymore. Things weren't going at all the way they had planned.

"You talk about grief being a process," one woman said, "and I can understand that. But what I don't understand is where I am in the process and how far I have to go."

We were all in the same boat. Each of us felt lost and in need of a milestone. We had been picked up by a whirlwind and dropped into an unexpected realm. And there was no yellow brick road to follow through the chaos. There was only the slow layering of our own experiences. Where we were and how far we had to go was a function of where we wanted to go, and this meant that some decisions had to be made. Making decisions is the first step in the process. Choices have to be made. You can learn to be self-sufficient, you can mooch off a relative, you can remarry. It hadn't been easy for me to begin making my own decisions after fifteen years of marriage, and most of the women in the room had been part of a pair for twice that time. All of us had to choose a direction for ourselves and begin taking steps toward our new futures. First a choice, then a step, then another, and little by little the journey itself would become the process. There wasn't any one way that was right for all of us. Each way was unique and each way was made by going in a direction we chose day by day.

"It's really something to see so many other people in my position," another woman said. "I felt better the minute I walked into this room. I felt less alone. See, I have a terrible problem just finding someone to do things with. I like to eat out, but I don't want to go by myself. What happened to all my old friends? Why did they drop me like a hot potato or something?"

Or something. Something like a bad person whom God has singled out and punished. Something like a dangerous person who has been tainted by her contact with disease, pain, and death. Something like a desperate, voracious woman on the prowl. Something like a threat. She hadn't just lost her husband. She had lost her place in society, and so had everyone else in the room. We all agreed to add our neighborhood to our name tag so we could find someone convenient to call and do things with. After all, *we* hadn't died. Not yet.

"My husband died seven and a half months ago," a young blond blurted out, "and I'm worried about my son. He's only six years old and he's so lonesome for his father that he turns to any man who comes along. I'm really worried that something terrible will happen to him. He's so trusting. How can I watch him all the time? How can I protect him from something terrible?" Then she burst into tears.

Forget the kid. What about Mommy? Chances are that junior would stick to gym teachers and scout leaders. He's no dope. The kid wouldn't be charmed by a weirdo, deviate, or bullshit artist, but you can bet your boots that Mommy would. And probably more than once. She was lonesome for his father, too. Only in her case it was a lot more complicated. She had lived with him for years. She had planned with him, despaired with him, encouraged him, argued with him, eaten with him, and slept with him. And suddenly he was gone and she was left. She was hurt, lonely, and scared. She was also getting horny.

"How could I be thinking about *that* already?" another woman asked. "Is it normal? He's been dead only a couple of months, and I'm embarrassed to say this, but all I can think about is sex."

"I'm sixty years old," said another, "and I'd like to know how to behave with a man. It used to be so different. It used to be like this. You went out with someone. You got to know each other. You made plans. You waited. Then, if he was a serious person, he gave you a ring and you got engaged. Now it's like this. You go out. He buys you a bagel at a deli, and—bang—he expects, already. So I'm afraid to go out. I'm lonely, but I don't know how to behave anymore."

Did any of us? We were all emotionally vulnerable. We were also out of touch. It had been decades since we last dated. We were confused by our sexuality, and we would be cannon fodder in the sexual revolution until we began to distill what was real from what was a fear or a fantasy. If we didn't understand what our own limitations and our own needs were, we would always have to settle for satisfying someone else's needs.

"He took care of everything for me," the Chinese woman finally spoke up. "Everything. A roommate. Does anybody need a roommate? Where do I find someone who needs a roommate?"

Is there wife after death? Can we find a warm familiar niche to crawl into? Can we sell ourselves "as is"? I have yet to open the newspaper and find a classified that reads:

Wanted, experienced wife. Woman between 20 and 80. Seven days a week. No holidays. Clean. Neat. Cheerful. No particular skills necessary. Employer will provide room, board, pocket money, car, credit cards, medical and dental, occasional sex.

"I'm a widow for the second time," a serious and attractive woman said. "I remarried a few months after my first husband died, and I never went through a grieving process. Years later, I totally fell apart. I was very unhappy with my marriage and with my life. And now that my second husband has died, I realize that I never gave myself a chance to understand or recover from the loss of my first husband. I found another marriage to jump into, and by doing that I didn't have to acknowledge that anything had happened and that anything was different. And I would like to give some advice to everyone here. Take your time. Grieve your loss. You can't make a meaningful commitment until you know who you are. Even though my second husband was a wonderful man, I wasn't happy with him. I should never have made such an important decision until I was emotionally stable. It wasn't fair to him and it wasn't fair to me. You can't re-create what you had. It's a mistake to try."

The workshop was a success. Women were talking to each other. Women were asking questions, giving advice or sympathy or encouragement. They were talking openly about very personal things and finding out that they were not weird or foolish. They were not alone. We had all been wives and we had all become widows. The next step was the step back to life, the step back to being a woman, and the quality of that step wasn't up to fate or luck. It wasn't up to what a husband did or how much he made. It was up to each of us.

18

They almost ran out of seats on the early-bird flight to Atlanta. There was an endless pile of nonrevenue standby tickets on the agent's desk, but mine finally appeared and I was given a boarding pass. So many people were involved in the planning and construction of the new airport that even with company business priority, even with a 5:40 A.M. check-in, I was almost bumped from the 6:20 flight.

I knew half the people on the airplane. They were from marketing or computer science or advertising, and we had all become buddies since the onset of the Atlanta Midfield project. A brand-new language had evolved between us that no one else could understand. There were meetings with DOA and HOH, there were problems with absorbing SOC 7 and NOB 4, and there was the steady, unflinching encroachment of DBO. We wore little green badges that identified us as members of the new fraternity within the fraternity. Whatever we needed we got. Whatever the project required we were prepared to give. There was an excitement generated by the sheer size of the job. It was the largest construction site in Atlanta, the biggest airport in the world, the greatest show on earth. And the countdown had begun. There were three months left to complete the miles upon miles of construction. In three months we would have to absorb an outgrown facility into a new location out in the middle of the airfield, where a sprawl of concrete waited to be ordered into a functioning port.

We were up over the city before the sun. The street lights still decorated Miami and a rhythmic grid sparkled below us for a moment. Then we cut through the clouds and lifted up into the dark silent sky. It seemed like ages since my first flight to Atlanta. I worried then about what to do with 200 square feet of facilities. A year later I had 450,000 square feet of responsibility and a lot less apprehension. It was more than "what the heck." That philosophy had been replaced by the gradual but continuous accumulation of experience. I knew what I had to do. It was thrilling to be able to do it.

"It is essential to the company that we finish this project on time," the vice-president had said to me, "and I want you and your people to devote as much energy and time as is necessary to get it done. The success of the airline is dependent on this facility's being ready to operate in September. Your predecessor got it started, and it's up to you to carry it off. You're really very lucky to have the opportunity to be involved in such an important project."

Had I missed the first flight out of Miami, I would have waited for the next one or flown to New Orleans and then up to Atlanta. Had I missed my lift to the site, I would have gotten some manager to drive me over, or I would have called a taxi, or I would have walked across the ramp and out to the middle of the field. I wouldn't have lost the day for anything. My carryons were jammed under the seat in front of me. I had a change of clothes and three binders filled with plans, studies, lists, orders, and invoices—the entire interior packet for the new Atlanta airport.

"It's just like a little project," my predecessor had said when he briefed me on Midfield. "It's just exactly like a little project, only bigger. Don't let the size scare you. There's nothing to it. Just think of it as one of your regular small jobs and multiply it by a hundred. The size shouldn't change or complicate anything you do."

"Someone once told me that about having another kid. They said that it would be the same as having one only multiplied by two. And do you know something, it was bullshit then and it's bullshit now."

"Oh, well, you use me as an excuse for six months. That's customary."

Three of the months had passed. My colleagues and I had already researched, designed, laid out, specified, and monitored the orders for everything that would go into the space our airline would occupy. That had been the easy part. The hard part, the fit-up, the race for completion, the last inch, was yet to come.

It had been a year since I had sat sweating on a 727 without any idea of what I was doing. A year ago I had been overwhelmed by the feeling of chaos in every aspect of my life. There was the new job and the house and the kids and the increasing complexity of every relationship and friendship. I had been overwhelmed by grief and guilt and anger and ambivalence. I had had so little time to think about it all, to sift through the confusion and figure out what I had to do to rebalance myself. I had only had those hours at 30,000 feet, cruising between places and between steps. That had been my space above it all, my "widow's walk," where I could just stop and look down and see what was what. The panic, the chaos, the ambiguity had been replaced by a fragile sense of order. Step by step I had reordered my life, and that was the way I survived the death of my husband and my marriage. So I wasn't sweating Atlanta. I wasn't sweating supporting myself or raising three kids or making new friends or living alone. I still felt terribly sad and empty, but at least I wasn't sweating.

The sun appeared from nowhere. The clouds broke up, revealing the flat fields below us. We were somewhere over Florida, but soon the landscape would change and we would begin our descent. A massive construction site would greet us. It would still be a plan, but step by step the confusion of concrete, steel, glass, cables, ducts, pipes, and wires would be transformed into a place, a grand central transportation station. In three months it would be orderly and safe and efficient. And it would work.

19

My assistant was marching down the empty concourse pulling her "wheely," the baggage cart that held our Atlanta Midfield files. A whistle hung around her neck. She used it to attract attention in the half-mile straight stretches of construction. A voice didn't go very far in the long, carpeted corridors. When I first saw the concourses that we had to finish, I was astonished. They were so long.

"I think I can see the curvature of the earth," I told the project architect. "My God, just think of the money we could make if we could figure out a way to get a roller skate concession in here."

My assistant had sores on her feet from walking up and down the concourse. She soaked them every night at the Airport Holiday Inn, where we were all staying. She was heading down the empty concourse to make sure that everyone was doing all the things that had to be done to get us one day closer to opening. I could count the days we had left on my fingers. The interior designer was rearranging furniture and hanging art work in the VIP club room. The

paint was still wet when the furniture was moved in. We had
been so anxious to see how the room would look that we
started placing furniture early. One of the contractors had
called us about the room the week before.

"I'm sorry to be bothering you and holding things up. I
know you folks are in a hurry, but I have never in my whole
life seen anything like this. I've painted a whole lot of walls
in my time, but I just wanted to check with you before I go
any further. I just want to make sure that I got the right
color before I go ahead and paint ten thousand square feet
of this here titty pink."

The interior designer told the project manager not to
worry and that everything would come together when the
furniture was arranged. But the sight of all that pink made
everybody so nervous that we began to wonder if we had
blown it. We hadn't. It looked great once the furniture was in.

In the morning I was sitting at a drafting table updating a
punch list for the seven o'clock meeting. The list was down
to two sheets of paper, but it was still too long. We were
racing against time, running on pure adrenalin. Even if
everything went smoothly it would have been difficult to
finish.

And nothing went smoothly. The general contractor ran a
plumbing stack right through the middle of a holdroom. The
sinks we specified for group rooms didn't work because they
weren't attached to the pipes. They weren't attached to the
pipes because there weren't any pipes to attach to. The
gates were misnumbered on all the signage. Our VIP rooms
were in violation of the health code because they didn't have
three sinks at the bar. The furniture was being stolen before
we could install it. The carpet was beginning to unravel and
no one could figure out how to get the construction dust off
the ramp. We had counted on the seasonal rain but had been
hit with a drought.

Every morning we met at seven and again at five in the

afternoon to say where we were and what we had left to do. No matter how much we did each day, the lists got longer as one problem after another popped up. There were so many errors and omissions to correct that I kept expecting someone way up like the director of aviation or the mayor of Atlanta or the governor of Georgia or the president of the United States to say, "Stop. Halt. Hold the show. You gotta be kidding. You gotta be out of your mind. This can't open. Hell, no. This can't work."

None of our computers worked because somewhere along the one hundred fifty miles of computer cable there had been an error or an omission. The baggage system didn't work because the programmer never wrote the program. He couldn't figure out how, but he had kept trying right up until the month before the airport was scheduled to open. Then he finally let us know that he was stumped and that he really hadn't done diddly. The roof leaked, and if the roof leaks when it isn't raining, you know you have a problem. The insulation for the air handling system had been omitted. There were errors in calculation too, so that in some places the air pressure was blowing out the ceilings. Errors and omissions, plague and pestilence, death and destruction, a week to go.

At the end of the day we all piled into Billy's Bar and continued working. Each airline claimed its corner. We ate nachos and talked strategy. We sent envoys to the other corners of the bar to try to find out how our competitors were doing and how they were solving problems. We tried to worm information out of city officials who wandered into Billy's looking for a free drink. As we ate nachos, we drank, and the more we drank the more creative we became.

"Hey, I know how we can clean up the ramp," one engineer said after his second margarita. "See, we get a van and we drive around Atlanta at about five in the morning. We drive around past all the parks and stores and stuff and we fill up the van with winos. Then we take them to the site and get them all brooms and tell them to start sweeping. At the end of the day we give them each a bottle of Thunderbird and let them pass out under the building. Then we wake them up the next morning and tell them to start sweeping again."

After a few more drinks we began to work on some problems that weren't on anyone's punch list.

"At least one representative from every airline that serves Atlanta has screwed this one secretary," said the project architect, "and you all know who I mean. Except for us. And I am personally tired of hearing our company referred to by everybody in the industry as the Virgin Airlines. It's humiliating. So, who's gonna do it? Who's gonna be man enough to save our pride?"

"Well, count me out," I said.

"My wife would kill me."

"I'm so nervous about completing everything on time that I can't even get it up anymore. You can ask my wife. You can ask anybody."

"Well, let's draw straws. Whoever gets the shortest straw . . . maybe it should be the longest straw. Yeah, whoever gets the longest straw has to do it. And that includes you too, Bonnie. You're the one who wanted to do a man's job. You're the one who thought being a woman wouldn't limit your activity at all. So, you gotta be prepared to carry out your obligation to the company. Now, whoever winds up with the longest straw has to get her in the sack before the first plane lands at Midfield."

The first airplane would land at Midfield in six days. The first airplane would touch the ground and the first agent in the control tower would tell the pilot which of the one hundred fifty gates to pull into. The first mechanic would usher it to the gate and a loading bridge would stretch out to receive it. The first passenger would walk out into the brand-new concourse and make his connection or find his way to the main terminal. The baggage would be distributed. A transportation system would move everyone under the miles of ramps and taxiways. Flight screens would display information, tickets would be sold, passengers processed, flights filled, messages received, problems handled, newspapers sold, drinks served, air conditioned, garbage collected, toilets flushed. And nobody who passed through would think twice. Nobody would marvel that it worked. If it worked.

Six days were left. In a few hours it would be five. We had to have our facilities ready, because the airport was really going to open on time. It said so in the newspaper. It said so on television. Nobody way up seemed to think it couldn't be done, so we would have to do it. All the highways would be rerouted at midnight on September 21. All the maps would be changed. There would be no other place in Atlanta to land commercial jets. Any airline that wasn't ready on that day would not have a plane in the sky.

Five days were left. The project controller didn't show up because he had had a heart attack the night before. His wife called from the hospital. He had been hired to replace a guy who was out because half of his ulcerous stomach had to be removed, who had been hired to replace another guy who left to work on a new airport in Saudi Arabia. The project manager had a hernia, but acted as though it were about as serious as a hangnail. If we weren't done in time we couldn't fly.

Four days to go. I ambushed the sign contractor at six-thirty in the morning outside his trailer and followed him around with tears in my eyes until he promised me that yes, he would take care of our signage problems the first thing that day. Yes, he would see that the gates were finally numbered correctly, and yes, he would get the right airlines listed on the right concourses, and yes, he would get the location here-you-are maps mounted, and yes, he would have removed the information sign that pointed to the station manager's private office. And yes, I would have a drink with him the very next time I was in Atlanta.

Three days to go. Four hundred men were out there sweeping the ramp. We hadn't picked them up directly off the streets. We had hired them from a temporary employment agency, but there they were, the winos with brooms, four hundred strong. And the ramp was getting clean. The other airlines had hooted with laughter at the first sight of our broom brigade, but after the second day of progress they were down in the dust trying to talk the gang into hitting their ramps next.

Two days to go. We couldn't locate the accessories for the VIP club. They had been flown into Vendor-Receiving at the old terminal and were floating around somewhere between Receiving and Material Distribution. The interior designer and I grabbed a station wagon and drove across the ramp and past the guard and over the active taxiways of the old airport to the freight hangar. It took us two hours to locate and load up the boxes of ashtrays, wastebaskets, sculpture, and artwork. I zipped back across the runway, yapping to the designer about how we had to do everything ourselves until I heard him whisper, "Oh, shit." I looked up and saw this big silver mountain coming toward us. An L-1011 on its way to take off.

Well, officer, I just didn't see him coming. He appeared from nowhere. I must have a blind spot. I wasn't speeding or anything, no, sir. What am I doing here? Well, sir, I was picking up some ashtrays and sculptures so we could get the new airport open on time. No, I haven't been drinking. I just didn't see him coming. He appeared from nowhere.

I accelerated and we made it by. The shadow of the wing passed overhead, and I'm sure that there is a tape in a black box somewhere that would have to be very heavily edited for public broadcast.

One day to go. The computers were up. A million-dollar pre-engineered metal building had been erected for the sorting of baggage until the final system would be completed. The air handling system had been adjusted and insulated. Two extra sinks had been squeezed into the VIP room, and you could have eaten off the ramp. My goal was to finish everything I had to do and catch the 5:00 P.M. flight back to Miami. I had been excused from the move and wanted to get out of Atlanta before it started. I had no desire to witness the six hours of insanity that would follow as every airline tried to move in its desks, chairs, trucks, carts, tricherators, battery chargers, coffee pots, wastebaskets, files, and pencil sharpeners and put them in place before the doors opened for business at 6:00 A.M.

My punch list was down to a few items. I ran through the terminal and checked out each room. Every stick of new furniture was in place. Every sign was hung, every wall was painted, every gate set up and ready for action. At 3:30 I changed into a dress and went to see the vice-president.

"Everything I can do is done. If there isn't anything else, I'd like to get home."

"Well," he said, "I noticed that the information sign pointing to the station manager's door is still up. He says he won't move into an office marked 'information,' and I can't say as I blame him. So, see that the sign is taken care of and then you can leave. Thanks for your help."

The sign man had failed me. He had missed one. One damn sign. I would never find him in time. I would miss the 5:00 plane, and if I didn't make that flight I would get caught up in the move. I would get swept up in the throng of vice-presidents, directors, and managers who would be running around the airport in a psychotic frenzy, armed with speedy memos and walkie-talkies.

I looked up and down the concourse and halfway down toward the transfer point I spotted my knight on a white horse—a workman on a ladder changing light bulbs.

"Oh, sir, could you do me a favor?" I asked. "Could you get up to that sign and remove the arrow, please?"

"I'm not supposed to touch those signs without a work order, lady."

"Well, consider this a work order. It's terribly important and you're my only hope."

"Look, lady, I don't know who you are, and I'm not supposed to touch those signs."

"Could I borrow your ladder then, please?" I took off my heels and climbed up the ladder. It was 3:45. I tried to peel off the vinyl die cut letters, but they wouldn't lift. "Do you have a knife or a razor blade I could borrow for a minute, sir?" I asked the man who was staring up at me.

He passed me a pocket knife and I began scraping. I scraped at the arrow that pointed to the manager's office. It didn't budge. It was 4:00 and I wanted to go home. I began to gouge at the sign. I wanted to see my kids. I wanted to sleep in my own bed. I wanted to go home. I pulled out a bigger blade and attacked the six inches of white vinyl arrow with the frenzy of Jack the Ripper. I was sweating in my silk dress. I wanted to go home.

"Hey, lady, you know something? You're defacing city property."

"No shit." I hacked the sign face. The arrow began to lift off. By 4:15 it was a pile of plastic on the floor below me. I climbed down, put on my heels, returned the knife, and ran down to the ramp. The project architect was waiting in the station wagon, and he drove me across the field to the airplane.

"Will standby passenger Liss please check the desk."

I hurried over to the agent at gate 5, who handed me a boarding pass.

"You're 1A," he said with a smile. "Have a good trip."

I thanked him and rushed to board the L-1011 that would take me home. The new terminal was ready to open. It had been a photo finish.

The airplane started down the runway and lifted off the ground with a strange grace. I looked out at the empty ramps of Midfield. Soon they would be alive with activity. In twelve hours the biggest airport in the world would be open for business. The completion date would be met. It had been set three years before and the job was done to the day and to the dollar.

I was exhausted and I was relieved. And I was crying. Tears were falling onto my dress and they just wouldn't stop. Nobody noticed me, though. They had their magazines and their drinks and they didn't notice that the lady in 1A couldn't stop crying.

Okay, it's okay, I thought. You're tired, it's over, it's okay. You're just tired. It's okay.

But there was something else going on. I had that old hollow and disconnected feeling. It was not okay. What was wrong with me? My life was in order. I was successful. I was able to support myself and three kids. My job was interesting and prestigious. I was confident and decisive. They could have featured me in *Savvy* or *Ms.* magazine. Except that I was slobbering into my screwdriver.

Goddamn it, Goddamn it, I miss him.

I didn't want to go home alone and take care of my kids alone and eat alone and brush my teeth alone and get into bed alone. The tears kept falling. So I had done a good job. So fucking what? That just wasn't enough. It was only a job. It was a neat job, okay, but it was only a job. It wasn't something I did just to do it. If they stopped paying me I sure wouldn't do it anymore. What was it I did because I flat-ass had to? What was it I did that made me make sense? Was there anything left that I loved to do? Was there anything that I would fight to do?

There were the kids. There were the kids. I had kept my family together. I nurtured them as best I could. But I wanted more. I had more once, and I knew that there was more. I wished that I were back up on the ladder, hacking at that arrow. I would have liked knifing that sign some more. I would have clawed straight through the anodized aluminum face and kept on clawing.

I didn't want to be alone. I didn't need to be taken care of anymore, but I did need to be enjoyed, to be applauded, to be loved. And I needed someone to love. It was as simple as that. I was crying because there was this absolutely necessary piece that was missing.

Okay, the job was great and the book had gotten good reviews. Okay, I had new friends, a terrific new baby-sitter, and money in the bank. Okay, the kids were growing up strong and fine. But, Goddamn it, Bob shouldn't have died. He was too young, and I'm not ever going to forget that. I'm a big tough girl, and I'll stop bawling and go home and keep right on being big and tough, but he shouldn't have died. That was unfair and awful. That was shitty and cruel. He shouldn't have died. I have to admit, God was wrong about that.

Asher opened the door when I got home.

"Whadja get me?" he asked.

"Damn it, Asher, is that all you can say? Can't you say hello and help me get my bags in?"

"Okay, sorry, Mom. Hello. Whadja get me?"

I put down my bags on the stoop and fished in my briefcase for one of the Atlanta Hartsfield Airport back-to-school pencil cases that I had managed to find at the closeout sale of the old airport gift shop.

He took the case and said, "Boy, you call this a present? Is this all you got?"

"Yes, Asher, that's all I got. You're lucky to get anything. The airport was about to close, and all they had left were pencils and porno magazines."

"Yeah. Well, this is a dumb present."

"Yeah. Well, you're a pain in the ass."

I dragged my bag in past him and through the television room, which was carpeted wall to wall with crumpled Dorito bags, empty soda cans, and three days' worth of the *Miami Herald*. Seth met me in the living room.

"Hi, Mom. Can I sleep over at Jimmy's? I finished all my homework and there isn't any school tomorrow."

"I just came home, Seth, for Christ's sake. Could you stick around for a few minutes? I might forget what you look like."

"Oh, please, Mom, please."

"I know, I know. His mother said it was okay. But your mother—remember her, the one with the curly hair and the suitcase?—your mother says it isn't okay." I handed him a pencil case, and he slumped off.

"You're so mean," he said when he was out of swatting range.

I ran into Miles in the hallway. "You're taller than me," I said. "When the hell did that happen? How did you get taller than me? Goddamn it, Asher's an absolute ingrate, Seth thinks I'm mean, and you're taller than me."

"Sorry, Mom. I guess there's no point in asking how your trip was."

I sat down on the steps and he sat next to me. "I don't suppose you want this," I said as I handed him the last pencil case.

"Sure, I'll take it. I need one for school."

"I probably should have gotten you a porno magazine. They still had some left."

"No, that's okay. I can use a pencil case and Peach left us plenty of porno magazines. Mom?"

"Yeah."

"Do you want to go play racquet ball?"

"Miles, are you nuts or just totally insensitive? Can't you see that I'm exhausted? I'm a complete zombie. I've been walking up and down these mile-long concourses for weeks. My feet hurt. My head hurts. I've been drinking heavily at high altitudes. The absolutely last thing in the world I want to do right now is play racquet ball."

"Sorry." He got up. "I'm sorry I asked. You don't have to be so bitchy. Just say no like you always do. A simple no would have been enough, Mom."

He left and I was alone in the hall on the steps. I looked into the hallway mirror and saw myself. My shoulders were hunched over and my hair was limp and shapeless. My face was drained of color. I looked like an artist's rendering of the Neanderthal woman. I wanted to cry some more, but I was too tired. Sandy, the baby-sitter, came in and stood between me and my reflection.

"Do you want a cigarette?" she asked.

"Sandy, you know I don't smoke. I'd love one."

"How did it go?" she asked.

"Okay, I guess. We finished. Tomorrow morning Atlanta will have a new airport."

"You do all right, Bonnie."

"Yeah, I suppose I do all right for a dumb, mean lady who looks like shit. I suppose I do all right."

"Well, you don't have to worry about dinner. I gave the kids that chili you left."

"What chili?" I asked. "Sandy, that was spaghetti sauce."

"Oh, no wonder."

"No wonder what?"

"No wonder it kept sliding off the fork. I went through two boxes of saltines just to firm it up enough to eat," she said, and we both started to laugh.

"Oh, God, don't make me laugh. It's been so long since I laughed that I might pull something. Were there any calls?"

"No."

"None of my fans called?"

"No."

"What about the man of my dreams. Did the man of my dreams call?"

"No, Bonnie," she laughed again, "nobody called. Oh, wait a minute. There was a call from—what was his name —oh, yeah, Raul. He said he got your check and he cashed it, and you should call him to set up a date for the closing on that piece of land."

So the lot was mine. I was now the owner of a piece of land on one of the original residential islands that frame Miami Beach and form a neighborhood in the bay. On it I could build a new house of my own design for me and the kids. It would be for the me who worked at a demanding job and didn't stay home to make sure that everything was just right for someone else. It would be for the me who needed a simple oasis at the end of the day, for the me who didn't do windows or floors or bathrooms or kitchens or dishes anymore. And it would be for the kids who were alone a lot and helped out and took care of themselves more and more all the time.

"What kind of house will you design for yourself?" Sandy asked.

"Oh, gee, well first of all it has to be as maintenance-free as possible," I said. "Sometimes I think all I really need is a cave with a high-pressure hose, but I'm soft and I want other things too. Things that keep out the rain and let in the breezes. Things that provide hot water and ice cubes and a machine that washes clothes."

"Well, I'm sure you have some good ideas about the kitchen. That's probably the most important room. I'd like to see a kitchen designed by a woman."

Now that was strange. I hadn't even thought about the kitchen. I had thought about the living room and how it would be the heart of the house and not a shrine to Ethan Allen. It would be open to the activity of the family and open to a garden and to the breezes and the sun. It would be a place where you could sit with a drink and maybe with a friend and feel comfortable and alive. I had thought about my bedroom and how it would be for all the quiet, private things. It would be my place to read, to write, to bathe, to rest, and to wake up and feel the energy and excitement of a new day. I had thought about the kids' area and how it needed to be in its own separate pod so my prime communication with them would no longer have to be "turn it down." I wanted it to be somewhat spartan and easy for them to take care of and flexible enough to accommodate them and their friends as they grew up and became young men.

But I hadn't thought about the kitchen. I used to think a lot about kitchens. I used to want a big country kitchen with lots of work area and a desk for planning meals and clipping coupons. I used to think that it would be neat to have a work island in the middle with a bar and pull-up natural bentwood stools on one side, butcher block and appliances on the other, and lots of copper pots hanging from the ceiling overhead. I used to want elaborate racks for wine and spices and a cleverly situated cork wall for messages and shopping lists and snapshots of the kids.

"You know something, Sandy, I don't think a kitchen is all that important. I mean, of course there has to be a place to store food and fix a snack. But when I want an elaborate meal, when I want a feast, I'm sure as hell not going to cook it—not after a day of work, not when I have just a few hours to divide between my kids and my friends. I don't even want a kitchen anymore. Who am I kidding? We'll eat out."

By nine-thirty I was in bed. The shower had cooled me down. My paddle fan moved the damp night air around me. I must have dozed off over a copy of *Progressive Architecture* when the phone rang.

"Bonnie, it's Henry. I'm glad you're back. If you're free this weekend, why don't we think about taking the forty-one-footer to Bimini, weather permitting, of course. Bring the kids if they want to come."

I woke right up. I felt excited and alert and ready for action.

"Wow, great. I'd love to. I've never been out of sight of land before. I mean, I've been out in the ocean, but I could always see the shore."

"Oh, there's nothing to it. I've been doing it for over thirty years. I've done it hundreds of times. I could do it in my sleep. In fact, I think I will do it in my sleep. You can sail us over. We'll leave Friday night at about ten, which should get us into Bimini at dawn."

"Is there a compass on the boat?" I asked.

"Yes, of course, but you don't sail by the compass. It's too boring, and staring at those damn numbers will make you seasick for sure. You have to check the compass from time to time and make adjustments, but you really sail by the clouds."

"But, Henry, the clouds move."

"Yes, they do, but they actually move very slowly. See, you pick a cloud and sail for it, and when you start to slip off course, pick another cloud and sail for that one. All the clouds are different, and they're just beautiful to look at.

They remind me of things—you know, old friends, places I've been, forgotten dreams. Just watch the clouds and sail and before you know it, you'll see the Bimini light, which means you are over the hump. And then you can forget the clouds and just go for the light and you're there."

KIDS HELPING KIDS
P.O. BOX 42398
CINCINNATI, OH 45242